More:
...You could'ner make it up!

All those Stoke City cup successes
(& the odd cup defeat)
that we don't half go on about!

Compiled by David Lee

LBA books

First published in Great Britain in 2009 by

LBA books
c/o www.impossibledreamers.co.uk
Stoke-on-Trent

A CIP catalogue record for this book is available from the British Library

ISBN 978-0-9541-2146-4

All characters and events in this publication are factual and real (no honestly they are), and
any resemblance to fictional persons, living or dead, is purely coinciden-...oh no, hang on,
that's not right. Oh, perhaps it is. Let's just say they're as real as it was possible to make
them without breaking them. I think that just about covers it.

Printed in Stoke-on-Trent by Wood Mitchell

Introduction
(The bit we daren't make up)

It is the summer of 1970, and the world is changing.

Things on the way out include:
- The Swinging Sixties (kind of obvious as it's 1970)
- Jimi Hendrix
- England from the World Cup for quite a long time (they blamed Peter Bonetti)
- The Labour Government (they also blamed Peter Bonetti[1])
- The Beatles (I don't think we can blame Peter Bonetti for this, can we?)
- Bradford Park Avenue FC (oh, they were just hopeless)

Things on the way in include:
- Moustached footballers
- The Wombles
- The Conservative Government (I blame Peter Bonetti, personally)
- Yoko Ono
- Power cuts
- and at Stoke City........Dudley Kernick?! (*Dudley Kernick*??!! Who the hell was Dudley Kernick??)

In his autobiography "*Who The Hell Was Dudley Kernick?*" (I'm not making this up, you know) Dudley describes his first day as commercial manager of Stoke City in July 1970, having joined them from Nuneaton Town.

---

[1] It is genuinely believed that Labour lost the general election in 1970 because England went out of the World Cup in the Quarter Finals four days earlier. Unfortunately, Peter Bonetti was in goal.

"Nothing ever happens..."

Before he's shown his office, which turns out to be just a concrete slab with a telephone beside it, Dudley runs into legendary Sentinel reporter Peter Hewitt, known as 'Mr Stoke City'[2]. Peter tells him "Don't worry, nothing ever happens at Stoke", and this is confirmed by his tour of the Stoke City trophy cabinet. The cabinet highlights included the Trent Vale Half-term Holiday Runners-up cup, a tatty Sentinel Shield Final pennant, a boomerang from Australia (no explanation forthcoming), a "blessing chair" from The Congo (just don't ask), and a freedom-of-the-city certificate from Cleveland USA for Stoke's heroic deeds as the Cleveland Stokers in the 1960s.

So, you can probably guess what this book is going to be all about: Stoke City seemingly never winning anything. Well, before 1970, that is. In those days Stoke were all chairs and boomerangs.

Bewildering picture of goalkeeper Peter Bonetti after conceding the goal that sent England crashing out of the World Cup. It is bewildering as Peter has actually signed it! Why would he do that? Bonetti was only playing that day as regular keeper, Stoke's Gordon Banks, was taken ill.

---

[2] Although Stanley Matthews, Denis Smith and Tony Waddington were also known, at one time or other, as "Mr Stoke City".

iv

A little unfair?

Even in early 1971, the equally unfulfilled Walter Pilkington (what a great name, eh?) was compelled to write an article in the Football League Review magazine about Stoke's limited fortunes. Headlined "A Little Unfair To Stoke?" Walter rather unfairly singled out Stoke City as a club that "had never won anything". HA!!!

Yeah, okay, so he had a point. Pre-1970 things had been a bit bleak. Even Walter struggled to remember Stoke's major claim to fame, which was winning the Second Division Championship… twice: once in 1933 (with the help of newly-signed Stanley Matthews) and again in 1963 (with the help of newly-signed …Stanley Matthews).

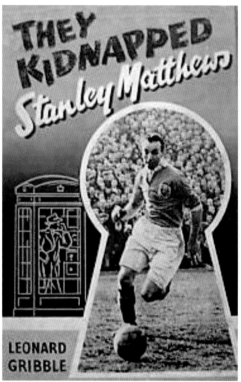

In fact taking into account their other stunning successes - the Third Division Northern Section championship of 1927, the Congo blessing chair and, of course, the boomerang – that's not a bad haul for 107 years.

Swine

But Walter was just being a swine. Why? Because he deliberately failed to mention Stoke's most glorious cup success of all time…well, up until 1970 anyway.

Yes, let's take you back in time to: …….

A wholly inexplicable novel, and not just an imaginative way to explain to potteries folk where Stan had been for 15 years

Ye olde FA Cup Semi Final against Derby County!

You must surely have heard of the legendary cup run of 1899?! A golden time, when Stoke smashed their way past the following superpowers of football:

- Sheffield Wednesday (then just called The Wednesday) by 2-0
- Birmingham City (then just called Small Heath) by 2-1, and
- Tottenham Hotspur (then just called "losers") by 4-1

Yes, it wasn't much of a cup run even for those days. Afterall, The Wednesday finished bottom of the First Division; Small Heath finished one place above Port Vale (then just called Burslem Port Vale) in the Second Division; and Spurs weren't even in the league at all at the time!

Ye olde FA Cup final at Crystal Palace park when everything was in black and white.

But it meant that Stoke only had The Rams between them and Wembley. Actually, that's not strictly true as the final was played in the park at Crystal Palace as Wembley Stadium hadn't been built in 1899.[3]

---

[3] The early FA Cup finals were played at Crystal Palace Park, not at Selhurst Park, as is commonly thought. Crystal Palace FC used to play at the Park, before being politely asked to leave the area by the military, whom you don't argue with. So they moved to nearby Selhurst.

The semi final was played at Molineux (home of Wolves), and the mighty Stoke City (then just called "Stoke") yielded a first half lead[4] to go down 1-3. They were taken apart by Derby-and-England's formidable centre forward, Steve Bloomer, who bagged a hat-trick.

The only consolation was that despite also taking a first half lead, Derby got trounced 1-4 in the final by Sheffield United. The only other consolation was that the Stoke players were given a £5 bonus each (worth about £500 in today's money).

When Stoke played against Derby's legendary Steve Bloomer it was like coming up against a brick wall

𝔓𝔬𝔰𝔱 - 1899

After that they had Stan Matthews to thank for a couple of 6th round appearances (1934 and 1946), and on both occasions Stan drew huge crowds. In the 1934 game against Manchester City, a record 84,569 filled Maine Road to see Stoke go down by a single goal. Before that there was the Arsenal 6th round drubbing in 1928 by 1-4.

Mind you, the 1928 cup-run was a huge improvement on the 1926/27 season, which was spent in exile (or in the Third Division North as it was also known). As such, Stoke suffered the indignity of competing in the *first* round of the FA Cup. There they faced the fairly un-scary welsh club Rhyl. After two 1-1 draws, they decided to settle the matter once and for all at Old Trafford, although God-knows-why as only 3000 fans turned up to watch Stoke throw away the lead to lose 1-2.

---

[4] Stoke's goalscorer was inside-right, Willie Maxwell. Apparently he's the last Stoke player to be capped by Scotland (just once). Now, there's a challenge for Tony Pulis, despite him being Welsh.

𝔖toke come first at something (1888)

P. HOLFORD.

Tom Holford, who played in many early Stoke disasters. He later became captain despite the 1970s moustache. Don't be fooled by his vacant appearance: Tom was allegedly known as "Dirty Tommy" Holford. The "P" is a mistake, and the bloke who made it is still in hiding

Many felt that Rhyl (1926) was the start of Stoke losing tragically to embarrassing non-league teams. Not a bit of it. They'd already done all that long before anybody else.

In October 1888, Stoke were said to have "unwisely" fielded their reserve side in an FA Cup qualifying round tie at home to Warwick County (who?)[5], and lost 1-2. Stoke thus became famous as <u>the first league club *ever* to be beaten by a non-league side in the FA Cup.</u> But there was more to this story than met the eye.

Firstly, as everyone knows, Stoke were one of the 12 founder clubs of the Football League. So, in this inaugural Football League season in 1888/89, Stoke had only been in the league for 28 days, as the Football League had only been going for 28 days, when they got knocked out of the cup. Sure enough, other league clubs were to fall to non-league opposition in the weeks that followed. However, Everton felt suitably insulted by the FA that they withdrew from the competition altogether, and Ulster went through to the next round in their place. So, in fact, it was Everton who went out to non-league opposition before Stoke did. OK?

Secondly, the FA had just introduced qualifying rounds. They did this to get rid of the minnows early (top club Preston had murdered Hyde 26-0 the previous season, which was thought to be a bit silly). But the FA decided that 4 of the 12 league clubs (including Stoke) should fight their way through <u>four</u> extra qualifying rounds. Only one of the league clubs, Notts County, made it through, only to be beaten by non-league The Wednesday.

---

[5] Warwick County's only claim to fame was that they played their home games at Edgbaston cricket ground. I wonder how long it took the cricket club committee to notice and boot them out!

Thirdly, there was a good reason for Stoke playing their reserve team: they'd decided, as many others would learn to do, to "concentrate on the league".

In fact they had no choice. The reason for this was that the FA had insisted that Stoke play their cup game on the same day as a league game! In those days the League was run by The Football League, and the FA Cup was (you guessed it) run by the Football Association. So it should come as no surprise that these two organisations should conspire to make Stoke, Bolton, Notts Co., (and Everton) play their qualifying cup games on the same days as league games.

So whilst Stoke reserves lost to Warwick, Stoke's first team were busy losing 0-7 at top club Preston North End. This was the famous game where 2 Stoke first teamers missed the train, and so two Preston reserves made up Stoke's 11 (no, honestly, it's true!). The 2 absentees (Alf Edge and "Greyhound" Sayer) at least got to play against Warwick, for all the good that it did.

Cover of yet another Stanley Matthews book. Stan didn't actually wear shorts. They were in fact white trousers that had ridden up in the wash.

Preston went on to win the double that season, Stoke finished bottom of the league (but weren't relegated), and Warwick County were expelled from the Midlands League after only one season, and were never heard of again (and quite right too). So it all ended happily in the end. But let's get back to 1970.

Getting back to 1970

Of course, since 1970 Stoke have in fact won quite a few things. This is just as well, as pre-1970 people could only associate Stoke with Stanley Matthews. He'd been there for almost all of their greatest successes; their 2nd Division championships (albeit 30 years apart), losing in the 6th round of the FA Cup a couple of times, and the acquiring of the boomerang (probably). This is in fact ironic as Stan's greatest successes were achieved elsewhere, for Blackpool and England.[6]

Yes, 1970!

So by 1970, it was definitely time for Stoke City to carve a new reputation. A reputation based on great cup wins and Dunkirk defeats. A reputation based on giant killings and giants squishing ants under their feat. It was time for action. So, in the wake of the 1970 World Cup, with the returning Stoke hero, Gordon Banks, the man who had made that greatest of saves from Pele, it just had to be 1970 that would be the start of a new chapter. 1970 had dawned, and a new era of cup glory was about to start. This is what 1970 meant to Stoke City!

Finally, 1970!

Actually, now I think about it, we'll start in 1964, if that's okay with you.

STOKE CITY
"THE POTTERS"
Victoria Ground

---

[6] I'm not doing anymore of these footnotes, coz they're full of rubbish and nobody ever reads them anyway. And what is this picture above trying to show? God knows.

X

STOKE DRAW 1-1 IN CUP FINAL!

Stoke City 1 Leicester City 1 (League Cup Final)

15th April 1964

WITH THE COMPLIMENTS OF **Ty·Phoo** LTD., BIRMINGHAM 5

STOKE CITY F.C.

Back row, L to R : F. Mountford (Trainer), Ritchie, Kinnell, Asprey, Leslie, Setters, Sherratt, Palmer, Allen, Bloor, A. Waddington (Manager)
Front row, L to R : Dobing, Vernon, McIlroy, Viollet, Matthews, Burrows, Skeels

When the guy from Ty-Phoo visited, the Stoke squad
all queued up for their free cup of tea

Hang on, Stoke City in the League Cup final. Surely you mean 1972?
Nope.

But surely you mean the final with Tony Waddington, Peter Dobing, John Ritchie, Gordon Banks and all that? Yes, this was the final with Tony Waddington Peter Dobing, John Ritchie, Gordon Banks and all that.

But Stoke won that final! Yeah, well, they drew this one.

So, Stoke made it to the 1964 League Cup final? Yes.

When did this happen? 1964!!!!!

Oh, right. But surely Gordon Banks hadn't joined Stoke by then? Duh! He was playing for Leicester, wasn't he. No wonder Stoke didn't win.

A Second Division club

How the hell did Stoke get to the final without him? Yes, now you're asking the right questions. After many years in the doldrums, Stoke had just got promotion to the top-flight, only to find themselves drawn in the League Cup against the mighty Scunthorpe United, at the time welded to the bottom of the 2nd Division with only 3 points, and not a win to their name.

Let me guess, it went to a replay? Nope.

It went to two replays? Yep. 2-2 away, 3-3 at home (Scunthorpe led three times), and 1-0 (finally) at Hillsborough in front of a measly 4,300 fans. This left just enough time in the fixture congestion to win 3-0 against Bolton Wanderers, at the time welded to the bottom of the 1st Division with only 7 points. Then Stoke got 3rd Division Bournemouth (2-1), and Rotherham (3-2).

What do all these games have in common? Rookie John Ritchie scored in every game!

Blimey. This was a real turkey-shoot! Er, yes. Finally, it was Manchester City, which sounds impressive, but at the time they were dawdling in the 2nd Division. Stoke cruised past them in a two legged semi-final 2-0 (Ritchie again) and 0-1 (not Ritchie again). They were through to their first national cup final in their 101 year history.

Wow! Good thing Stoke didn't meet any of the top teams on the way! Er, yes, that was a bit of luck.

I suppose Leicester beat all the big clubs?! Er, yes, that's right.

So who did they beat? Erm, Aldershot, Tranmere, Gillingham and Norwich.

They don't sound like very big clubs. Something's a bit fishy here, isn't it? OK OK! So the top-half of the 1st Division didn't bother entering, and the best of the rest (the likes of Chelsea and Blackburn) got knocked out at the first hurdle playing under-strength sides. Happy now?

What sort of second-rate…? Although the League cup had been started in 1960, most of the top clubs thought it was crap…until 1967 when the final was moved to Wembley and the winners got a place in Europe (in the brilliantly titled Inter-Cities Fairs Cup, which became the boringly titled UEFA Cup, and is now the weirdly titled

OFFICIAL PROGRAMME 3d.   № 3707

Telephone : Stoke-on-Trent 44660   FOUNDED 1863   Telegrams : "Football." Stoke-on-Trent

STOKE CITY

FOOTBALL CLUB (1908) CO. LTD.

Directors: G.W. Taylor, (Chairman) C.T. Salmon (Vice-Chairman) G. G. Crowe, F.R.C.S., T. L. Duddell, A. A. Henshall,   Manager: Tony Waddington   Secretary : W. C. Williams

STOKE CITY
Red and White Stripes   White Shorts

LESLIE

ASPREY (2)   ALLEN (3)

PALMER (4)   KINNELL (5)   SKEELS (6)

DOBING (7) VIOLLET (8) RITCHIE (9) McILROY (10) BEBBINGTON (11)

Referee :   Linesmen :—
W. CLEMENTS   C. F. Duxbury,
(W. Bromwich)   Yellow Flag
J. A. Roberts
Red Flag

STRINGFELLOW (11) GIBSON (10) SWEENIE (9) HEATH (8) RILEY (7)

CROSS (6)   KING (5)   DUGGAN (4)

APPLETON (3)   SJOBERG (2)

BANKS

Royal Blue Shirts   White Shorts
LEICESTER CITY

LEAGUE CUP FINAL—FIRST LEG

VERSUS

LEICESTER CITY

WEDNESDAY, 15th APRIL, 1964.   Kick-off 7-15 p.m.

In those days players had to play in the positions laid out in the programme, or else the manager didn't know where they were.

Europa League. Ugh!). But even then Liverpool still thought it was crap (but then they'd qualified for the European Cup anyway), and along with Everton (Cup Winners Cup qualifiers) they still couldn't be arsed to join in.

Did history prove them right? History tried to prove them right, when the first Wembley winner in 1967 in front of 98,000 fans was… Third Division QPR. To make matters worse, The Rangers were then controversially deemed too lowly to enter the Fairs Cup. So, yes, somewhere between second-rate and a complete joke. It was only in the late 1960s did it gain its credibility with teams like Arsenal and Leeds doing battle.

So, did Stoke stand a chance against Leicester in the final? Not really.

So Leicester were the better side? Don't be bloody ridiculous! It was just that Fate dealt a cruel blow to Stoke.

The reason why Stoke were destined to lose

You what? The Rulers Of Fate chant the following mantra, which all Stoke fans know to be true: "Verily, it is written that if Stoke City are in a cup final, and West Ham are beaten in the semi-final, then the team that puts out the Hammers wins the cup." Everybody knows that.

Don't tell me…: Yes, Leicester beat West Ham 4-3 and 2-0 in the semi-final. Stoke might as well as not turned up for the final.

But what actually did happen in the final? Well, the final was a two legged affair, and both matches were superb games of football. The Sentinel described the first game, played at The Victoria Ground, as "Pulsating", "thrills and excitement", and "30 years for great-train-robber Ronnie Biggs!" (oh sorry, that was another story that day).

So a real thriller? Yes! Apparently, Leicester were "raked by Stoke's fire". Don't know exactly what that means, but basically Stoke dominated most of the game. Peter Dobing hit the inside of the post, and John Ritchie's shot was cleared off the line, as Gordon Banks had corner after corner to contend with.

Who scored first? On 62 minutes Banks could only parry Bill Asprey's drive, and Keith Bebbington fired in off the underside of the bar for 1-0. But on 79 minutes, Eric Skeels' clearance rebounded to Gibson who equalised. 1-1. For the last 10 minutes, Stoke's defence clung on desperately.

What was the crowd like? 22,309, which is interesting.

Doesn't sound very interesting to me. Well, it is when you take into account that on the following Saturday 45,697 packed into The Victoria Ground to see Stoke beat Manchester United 3-1. In fact the papers were more interested in that game than the League Cup final.

How many saw the second leg at Filbert Street? 25,372 (including about 2000 Stoke supporters). And they saw another thriller.

Those were the days when you could buy a replica kit for only £1.60 from Ramsbothams

How was it decided? Well, apparently if it had been a draw, then they would have had to have had a "toss up for the cup" (well, that's what they said), as it was not possible to fit in a replay before the end of the season due to the worsening fixture congestion.

I meant how did the game go? End to end stuff, with both keepers (Banks and Bobby Irvine) performing heroics. Reserve keeper Irvine was in for Lawrie Leslie, who had been injured in the first leg.

I thought it was his ankle? OK, a twisted ankle in his first leg. But Irvine was Banks' equal that night. Despite Stringfellow putting Leicester 0-1 up after only 6 minutes, Stoke poured forward, with Ritchie hitting the bar. Just after the break, Jimmy McIlroy's long pass found Dennis Violet who beat Banks to make it 1-1.

What turned the game? Stoke's captain Calvin Palmer was carried off on a stretcher. With no substitutes, the trainers took 15 minutes to get Palmer back on. By this time, Gibson had made it 1-2 to Leicester from a corner. However, Stoke weren't going to go down without a fight, and with a rejuvenated Palmer, they pounded the Leicester goal. But when Riley made it 1-3 in the 83rd minute, it looked all over. However, a few minutes later, Palmer screwed the ball back for George Kinnell to blast home. 2-3 to Leicester, and a frantic finish ensued.

What really won the game for Leicester? In the last few minutes, the tireless Palmer put Ritchie through, and he let rip a blockbuster of a shot. But who else but Gordon Banks could pull off what The Sentinel described as "a save in a million", putting the ball round the post and effectively winning the cup for the Foxes.

After winning the League Cup, Leicester City commemorated the event with this handsome collectable coin set. Yuk!

What did the press make of that?? Great game, but now it's time to look forward to that exciting league match on Saturday... at Fulham.

Was it really forgotten that fast? Well, Stoke had just survived their first season back in the top-flight, had just beaten Manchester United and were about to draw 3-3 at the not-so-mighty Fulham! However, in the following week they beat league champions Liverpool 3-1 in their final match of the season to finish a respectable 17th.

But Stoke could have won a major trophy! It was generally felt that Stoke were unlucky to lose the League Cup final in 1964. They had afterall beaten

ALL of the top-5 clubs at the Victoria Ground in the league, but couldn't beat mid-table Leicester in the cup, mainly due to Gordon Banks.

Were Leicester more up for the cup? They were regular cup-finalists at the time, which is a nice way of saying they were good at getting to the final and then losing. This time they broke with tradition and actually won!

Did it lead to greater things? No. Leicester lost in the League Cup final the following year to Chelsea. They then lost in the 1969 FA Cup final to Manchester City, and a few days later were relegated. It was downhill all the way after beating Stoke.

But what if...? Things could have been very different. This could almost have been Stoke's "Stanley Matthews final". Stan had been injured in January, but was actually fit again by the time of the final. He even played the same night as the first leg at Bert Trautmann's testimonial at Maine Road. Moreover, Leicester's Frank McLintock (later the captain of Arsenal) failed a late fitness test and was left out injured for both games. We were going to hear more about him, no doubt about it.

And what happened to goalie Bobby Irvine? He later fell out with Tony Waddington who accused him of giving away a "stupid" penalty against Walsall in the FA Cup. After retrieving the ball, he decided to kick a Walsall striker who had been giving him stick all game. He didn't even get booked. Those were the days. The striker was none other than Allan "Sniffer" Clarke, who took his "stick-y" ways to fame and fortune with Leeds United. As for Irvine,

The great Northern Ireland international goalkeeper Bobby Irvine, who played the second leg (but deliberately kicked the first one).

he never played again, and the following year Waddington bought Gordon Banks.

STOKE BEAT EVERTON IN FA CUP FINAL!

Everton 2 Stoke City 3 (FA Cup Final)

7th May 1971

Eee eye addio, we won the cup! Er, no we didn't.

But it says that we won the FA Cup final, so we must have won the cup! Unfortunately, we won *"an"* FA Cup final, but not *"the"* FA Cup final.

It was a safe prediction that a team in red was going to win the cup that year.

Well, I don't remember them winning *an* **FA Cup final. Was it** *an* **FA Youth Cup final? Or** *an* **FA incontinent-old-gits Cup Final? Or…** No, you're way off. This was the proper FA Cup. But, you see, the FA ….were experimenting on us!

What, like the aliens did in the film *Close Encounters Of The Third Kind*? At this juncture I think it's just going to be easier for me to answer "yes", methinks.

Is it anything to do with Stoke reaching the FA Cup semi-final in 1970/71 for the first time in 72 years? I'd be impressed with this answer if you hadn't just looked that up.

So this is the great 1970 bit that we've all been waiting for?! Yes, it was 1970, when the country began to go to the dogs – oil crisis, 3-day week, power cuts, those droopy moustaches – after England's demoralizing return from the Mexico World Cup…

I blame Peter Bonetti… You can't blame

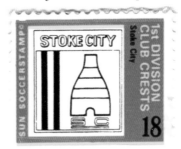

(© News Group Newspapers)

Peter Bonetti for the oil crisis.

Oh, alright then. Go on. Stoke were emerging as a major player in English football. Yes, I know that might be hard to believe, but it was true. Since 1964's cup final defeat, they'd survived seven seasons dawdling in the top-flight. But then they hired Alan A'Court (the Liverpool and England old boy) as coach, and signed a host of exciting new players.

Bet I've never heard of them. What about centre forward John Ritchie.

But he was already at the club for the last cup final. Ah, but in 1966 he'd been accidentally sold by Tony Waddington to Sheffield Wednesday. (He was told that Stoke needed the money to pay the players' wages!) Wednesday must have guessed he wasn't staying long as he never unpacked his suitcase, insisted on playing in red and white, and continued to commute from Stoke (sadly, only the latter part is true). Soon deemed to be over-the-hill, they sold him back cheap to Waddington, who was mightily relieved that his worst mistake had at least made some money. Ritchie went on to score loads more goals for Stoke.

OK, he was exciting, but not exactly new. Fine, what about Gordon Banks.

Big John Ritchie was forced to leave Sheffield Wednesday when it became clear that they didn't have a shirt big enough for him

He's not new either. He was in the last cup final too. Yeah, playing for the other side though. Ah, but lucky old Leicester City then had baby Peter Shilton (17), and they reckoned Banks (29) was over the hill, despite him winning the World Cup only the year before! Yes, THE World Cup.

What medication were *they* on? Something strong, obviously. Waddington got in & signed him before Liverpool could grab him. He was clever like that.

Who else did he pinch then? Superstar striker Jimmy Greenhoff, whom Waddington out-manoeuvred Everton for. Greenhoff was a product of Don Revie's cynically dull Leeds United (yawn). Deemed far too exciting for the club, he was squeezed out after winning the League Cup against Arsenal in 1968. Came to Stoke via a brief stop at Birmingham City. God knows what he

2 - 2

was doing there; he must have made a wrong turn on spaghetti junction!

Don't give up the day job. Who else? Well, there were several others.

In what way were there "several" others? Well, defender Denis Smith, although he was often broken into several pieces; left back Mike Pejic, although he was often suspended for several matches; and midfielder George Eastham, although he was often away coaching in South Africa for several months. One does wonder how Waddington used to put up with this lot!

So were Stoke now ready for a cup run? Yeah, about time too. Stoke hadn't been further than the 5th round for 25 years. Some felt it was because of what had happened the last time they were in the 6th round.

In 1946? In scenes not dissimilar to the Hillsborough disaster of 1989, 33 supporters died crushed by thousands of fans trying to get in to see the

17 year old Peter Shilton shakes hands with Gordon Banks after Stoke had beaten Leicester 3-1 in 1967 soon after Banks's transfer. A policeman hovers nearby in case of trouble!

Bolton vs Stoke cup tie. However, much to the horror of the players, this didn't stop the game being played! Although Bolton went through, they were subsequently beaten by Charlton in the semi-finals.

So were Stoke now ready for a cup run? Despite being used to going out to top clubs like Manchester United (1965 & 1967), West Ham (1968) and Chelsea (1969), Stoke had been upset 0-1 by lowly Watford in 1970. So there was little evidence of any cup greatness to follow.

Was there evidence of any cup greatness on the way to the semi-finals? Not a lot. Stoke came from behind to beat Millwall 2-1, sweet revenge on the second division side who had knocked Stoke out of the League Cup 4 months previously. They then took on newly-promoted 1st Division upstarts Huddersfield Town. Stoke had already done the double over them in the league. After 3-3 at home, and (3 days later) 0-0 away, Waddington struggled to find 11 fit players to go to Old Trafford for yet another replay. After 278 minutes of all this, Greenhoff scored the winner (1-0).

How did they get past the 5th round? It took another replay, this time against Bobby Robson's Ipswich (featuring future Stoke manager, Mick Mills). 0-0 at home, Denis Smith's thumping header was enough at Portman Road. 1-0.

Denis Smith?!? Yes, I know, a defender scoring the winner.

No, I don't mean that. What I mean is, how the hell was Denis Smith playing? Wasn't he broken in several pieces? Actually, that's a good point. This time he really was broken in several pieces. He'd broken his ankle during the Huddersfield marathon, and almost had his ear torn off

Happy Jimmy Greenhoff enjoying his year at Birmingham City

getting in the way of Frank Worthington's boot (blood everywhere, several stitches, carried on playing – a normal day for Denis, apparently). But a week later, he was patched up and scored the winner.

How the hell did he do that? By wearing a plaster cast during the week, and having a pain-killing injection before the game. Neat trick, eh? Don't try this at home, kids!

An easy draw in the 6th round? Hull City away sounded easy, but Terry Neill's side was top of the old Division 2 (promotion eluded them for decades till Phil Brown turned up). Stoke had to come from behind in a snow storm to win 3-2.

Worth it, though! Yep, it set up the infamous semi-final against lucky-lucky Arsenal.

STOKE CITY VS ARSENAL, FA CUP SEMI FINAL 27TH MARCH 1971

How lucky-lucky were Arsenal? Well, they hadn't been for ages. After not winning anything for nearly 20 years, they managed to scrape home to win the Inter Cities Fairs Cup, which it's claimed (unfairly) they only got into after losing the League Cup Final to Third Division Swindon (who were naturally ineligible). Now they were impulsively hunting the league and cup double, despite being miles behind Leeds in the league and being drawn against the mighty Stoke in the cup.

How mighty? Well, Stoke had already slaughtered them 5-0 a few months before. This time in front of a huge Hillsborough crowd, they looked like they were going to do it again. A Peter Storey clearance bounced off Denis Smith to give Stoke the lead, and then Charlie George (the one that everyone said wore a bra)(and walked like a woman)(fans can

"Charlie George, Subbuteo-star, Wore this red shirt on top of his bra!" (www.Soccerprint.co.uk)

be so cruel)(I think he did actually wear a bra though) made a weedy back-pass to goalie Bob Wilson, allowing Ritchie to slip in and make it 2-0. However, Greenhoff (amongst others) should've then gone on and buried The Gunners.

But they didn't, did they? No. In the second half Storey's shot was ironically deflected in off Smith, making honours even between these two. Then, a few hours into injury time (where the referee found 5 minutes of it, god only knows), Arsenal won a corner, despite Banks being blatantly fouled by George Graham. Captain Frank McLintock evaded Smith to head home, but it was fisted off the line by Mahoney (who wasn't down to play goalie that day).

Storey equalised from the penalty spot. It was so late by now that the linesmen had got changed and gone home. It was so late that BBC1 was playing the national anthem before closing down for the night. It was so late that milkmen up and down the country had started making their morning deliveries…

Yes, we've got the message. It was a bit late finishing, it seems, luckily for Arsenal. I don't like to go on about it but, well, we was robbed!

Is this the same Frank McLintock who'd missed the Leicester League Cup final 6 years before? Yes. He'd come back to haunt us for no real or apparent reason. That's the Scots for you.

But there was always the replay at Villa Park four days later? Unable to overcome their disappointment at Hillsborough, Stoke were never really in it. They never recovered from George Graham's early flying header, and Ray Kennedy (assisted by Charlie "bra-man" George) finished them off, 0-2.

Arsenal's goal was so late that Wembley had already printed the programmes for the final.

So how did they end up playing Everton? Usually the FA organised an England vs Young England game to be played on the eve of the cup final. But as it had, as they put it, "outlived its attraction" (ie. it was rubbish and no one came to watch), they decided to have a $3^{rd}/4^{th}$ Play-off final instead featuring the losing semi-finalists. Manchester United naturally drew a big crowd to win the first one in 1970. So now it was the turn of Stoke and Everton, who in turn had lost out in their semi-final to Liverpool.

So two very bitter teams? But a damn fine game though, despite being played Friday evening at Selhurst Park in front of only 5,031 supporters, compared with the 100,000 who would see Arsenal beat Liverpool 2-1 the following day.

Did they bother fielding full strength teams? They did actually, but Smith, Bloor, Dobing and Conroy were all injured, as was Everton's striker, Joe Royle. With a patched-up Stoke defence, Everton were 0-2 up in 17 minutes with an Alan Whittle header and an Alan Ball (later a Stoke manager, you may remember) volley. But Mike Bernard soon pulled one back (1-2). Then it was the John Ritchie show, as he tore The Toffeemen apart with a headed goal just after half-time and the winner ten minutes from time.

We were THIRD! Yes, Stoke finished 3rd in the FA Cup in 1971, just behind Arsenal and Liverpool. And you tell that to young people today…and they won't believe you.

Football Association Challenge Cup

3rd and 4th Place Play-off

Everton *v.* Stoke City

SELHURST PARK

Friday, 7th May, 1971
at 7.30 p.m.

OFFICIAL PROGRAMME 5p

No expense spared on the match programme

I'm not sure I believe it either. Well, to prove it actually happened, the winning players were all given small plastic medals …or was it tankards. Oh, who cares!

How did The Sentinel describe it? "Third place, after all, is still a highly credible achievement."

And how did Stoke fans describe it? "Selhurst Park on a Friday night? You must be bloody joking!" Mind you, they had just seen Stoke play their final league home game only *two* days before. Anyway, this 3rd/4th place lark wasn't going to last forever with crowds as low as 5000. Surely it would improve the following season.

Hm, we'll see. At least Stoke could get revenge on Arsenal by stopping them winning the League Championship? That's the spirit. Stiff upper lip and all that.

Well, did they? No.

What happened? The stiff upper lip went limp, and the season fell away. Stoke only won 2 of their last 11 league games, finishing mid-table, where they had been all season. Despite putting up a spirited performance against Arsenal, their penultimate game, The Gunners sneaked a 0-1 win, allowing them to overtake Leeds to win the championship by a point. And thus, they won the double.

So it was all our fault. I'm afraid so. On the walls of Highbury (before they pulled it down to build 700 apartments) were photos of the Arsenal heroes of that double-winning season: McLintock, Storey, Radford…and the Stoke City team. We'd have to have our revenge!

STOKE CITY'S GREATEST CUP FINAL TRIUMPH!

Stoke City 2 Chelsea 1 (League Cup Final)

4th March 1972

You're probably going to tell me that Stoke didn't actually win the League Cup in 1972, or that most teams didn't enter or were disqualified, or that it was the *Southern* League Cup, or... Nope, Stoke City really did win a major English football trophy. In the 1970s the League Cup was taken seriously, partly because there wasn't much else to win and partly because of the route to playing in Europe.

So it really was 12 games that changed the world? Not sure they changed the world, but they changed Stoke City. At last there was something to add to the mouldy pendant and the boomerang in the trophy cabinet.

If there were only 6 rounds (including the final) why did Stoke play 12 games? They just wanted to make it difficult for themselves. In the 1970/71 season they played 56 games. But in the 1971/72 season they played a total of 67 games! They were never mad enough to try doing this again.

So had Stoke signed loads of new exciting players?! Oh yes! Well, not really. George Eastham was back

Picture shows Southport inhabitants queuing to escape from the place

from South Africa, leaving his dad, George Eastham Snr, in charge. And Peter Dobing was back from injury and suspension. Er, that was about it, I'm afraid.

Had they prepared for a long run in the League Cup? Oh yes. Well, not really. This preparation entailed losing at the first hurdle for the previous three seasons to the likes of 2nd Division Blackburn, Burnley and Millwall.

So, did they draw an easy home game? No. They started their campaign in September 1971 at Haig Avenue, home of Southport FC (now in the Conference North League). They were big lads, and Stoke weren't at full strength – Gordon Banks, for example, was supposedly rested with an ear infection.

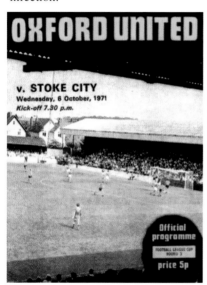

But it looked easy on paper! Stoke took an early lead – a rare goal from defender Alan "Bluto" Bloor, who ran the length of the field to belt the ball past a startled Southport keeper. Southport smartly equalised (1-1), but later conceded a penalty. However, after consulting the linesman, the ref changed his mind, and gave a free kick the other way! In the 70th minute, Greenhoff pounced on the loose ball in the box to knock in the winner (2-1).

Did they draw an easy home game in the next round? No, away to Oxford United (now in the Conference League). Again, Stoke took an early lead – Ritchie dispossessed the hapless Oxford keeper who "failed to see Ritchie" creeping up on him (how could you NOT see Big John Ritchie!), who slipped it to Greenhoff to do the rest. But a late equaliser for Oxford slid through a ruck of players to earn them a 1-1 draw and a replay at the Victoria Ground.

But it looked easy on paper! The rain-sodden replay had Stoke as the "walking-wounded", with strapped knees (Banks and Smith), broken toes (Ritchie) and groin strains (Greenhoff). Ritchie fired the Potters ahead, with Sean Haslegrave's late volley settling the matter at 2-0.

Ah, but I happen to know that Big Ron Atkinson, later manager of Manchester United and Aston Villa, was captain of Oxford at the time, where he was known as "The Tank". I bet he left his indelible stamp on these games! No.

Why not? He didn't play.

Oh. But his brother Graham did (he was a far better player than Ron anyway). And talking of United…

Did they draw an easy home game in the next round? No, away to Manchester United (now in the UniBond Premier League).

Are you sure? Oh, no, sorry, that's FC United Of Manchester, of course. Manchester United are in the *Barclays* Premier League. I always get those two mixed up. At the time United were top of the league, and on a roll.

Did United play their first team? If you mean Stepney, Kidd, Charlton, Law and Best, then yes they did. But Stoke pulverised them until eventually Ritchie blasted home in the second half. Although United equalised soon after (1-1), it was Stoke who got the standing ovation of the Old Trafford crowd.

Another replay? With a young Sammy McIlroy (later a Stoke star) in for Denis Law, United slogged it out with Stoke at the Victoria Ground, but despite extra time it ended 0-0. The teams limped off exhausted. But the best part was Tony Waddington flipping a coin.

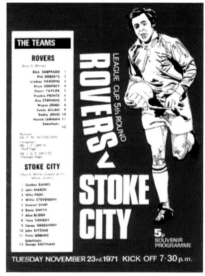

Why? Coz he won the toss and thus the second replay would be at the Victoria Ground. Another 40,000+ crowd saw the inspirational George Best open the scoring, and Dobing equalise in the second half. But it was super-sub Eastham who crossed for Ritchie to head home the late winner, and United were out.

What happened to United? They never recovered. From poll-position, they plunged down the league, and lunged from one cup defeat to another. Despite signing a young Lou Macari, they were relegated two years later; their last game ironically was losing 1-0 at the Victoria Ground, condemning them to Second Division football.

And so Manchester United's demise in the 1970s was all Stoke's fault? Well, partly. Well, quite a bit. Actually, yes, it was all our fault. OK?

Brings tears to your eyes. Yeah, tears of joy!

So, did they draw an easy home game in the next round? Don't keep asking that! No, they didn't; it was away to Bristol Rovers (now in the … well, the same division they are now; the Third Division, now called League One. Well that's 40 years of progress for you).

Can't imagine many people turning up for this mid-week league-cup game. Amazingly, nearly 34,000 filled Rovers' old ground that night, although the following year capacity was restricted to a third of this. Then they build a motorway across part of it, then it caught fire, fell down and then the club had to move away. It's now an IKEA store. Next time you drop in for a plate of meatballs, remember that Stoke played a tough League Cup quarter final there.

But it looked easy on paper! Actually, for once it did. Despite the appalling sea of mud that the game was played on, Stoke were soon 2-0 up with goals from Greenhoff and Denis Smith.

Was Smith in one piece for a change? Not for long. He clashed heads scoring the goal, and broke a couple of fingers. Concussed, he couldn't remember the rest of the game. After the break, cracking goals from Bernard and Conroy soon made it 4-0, although a sloppy consolation and then a very late penalty allowed Rovers the respectable scoreline of 4-2. On to the semi-finals!

So, did they draw an easy...? No! There were no easy opponents left. They were all from London: Chelsea, Spurs and West Ham. Cor, blimey, strike a light, up the apples and the pears, me darling!

Was that your best cockney? Yes, sorry about that. Anyway, Stoke were paired with The Hammers. What followed was one of the most extraordinary cup semi-finals of all time.

ONE OF THE MOST EXTRAORDINARY CUP SEMI-FINALS OF ALL TIME! STOKE CITY VS WEST HAM UNITED

Anybody famous in their team? Bobby Moore, Geoff Hurst, Trevor Brooking, Frank Lampard senior, and one Harry Redknapp.

So, anybody famous in their team? Suppose not. No ex-Stoke players, if you mean that. However, Redknapp, of course, went on to fame and fortune as Bournemouth's manager, working alongside the great Tony Pulis. As for Stoke's team, only Smith was absent, as he still didn't really know what day it was. (I think he thought it was apricot.)

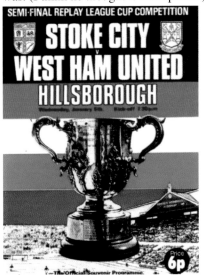

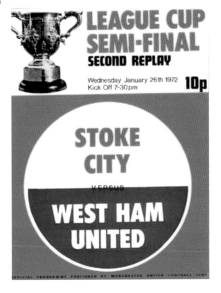

How did the first leg go? At the Victoria Ground, Dobing put Stoke 1-0 up, but Hurst's penalty equalised. Clyde Best made it 1-2. Not a great start.

How did the second leg go? At a soaked Upton Park, Ritchie finally squared the game in the second half, but late in extra time, Banks was judged to have knocked over Harry Redknapp. Well, strike-a-light, me old china!

Controversy follows that man around! It's his middle name. Frankly, it didn't look like a penalty, more like Redknapp falling over and grabbing at Banks. Hurst stepped up to take the penalty, but amazingly a fired-up Banks palmed it over the bar with a stunning save, one of the greatest of his career. 2-2 on aggregate. As there was no away-goals rule, it was another replay.

How did they find time for all these games? With difficulty, but the money was good. 47,000 watched the snowy 0-0 replay at Hillsborough. It was a great game with Stoke having the better of it. Denis Smith even put the ball in the back of the net!

Why wasn't it a goal? Because he put the goalkeeper in the back of the net as well. Naughty Denis.

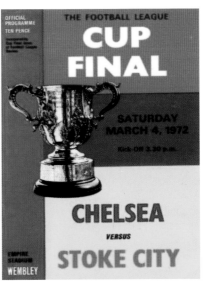

Did Waddo win the toss again? Yes, and so he decided to play the next replay at Old Trafford, a long way from London. [Please note: Tossing a coin or participating in any games of chance can lead to a betting addiction, and result in you wasting all your time and money on the bet365 web-page. Tony Waddington winning the toss twice was just luck, not a reason to take it up as a hobby or a life-pattern. I'm just saying, that's all!]

This one didn't look easy on paper! Seven weeks after starting this semi-final (no, really!), the teams met again in the cold and wet in front of nearly 50,000 fans. This time it was Conroy who collided with their goalkeeper, Bobby Ferguson, but this time he didn't get up.

Didn't they have a substitute keeper? They weren't allowed one in those days, so Bobby Moore went in goal, even though he might have been of more use outfield. After 30 minutes he saved a penalty, although Bernard put in the rebound. Billy Bonds' rocket of a shot cannoned off Denis Smith to make it 1-1. Goalkeeper Ferguson came back on just in time for Brooking & then Dobing to both score in the final seconds of the first half. 2-2.

Did they need a fifth game to sort this out? No. Terry Conroy finally hammered in the winner from a poor clearance early in the second half. West Ham had a goal disallowed, but Stoke clung on at 3-2 and were in the final!

Time for a song? I beg your pardon? Oh hang on, is this to do with Dudley Kernick again?

Who the hell was Dudley Kernick? Exactly. In his book, Dudley tells of the hit songsters, Tony Hatch and Jackie Trent, both keen Stoke fans. Tony had written hit songs and TV themes such as BBC's "Sportsnight". Jackie was from Newcastle-under-Lyme, describing herself as a "Bignall End Babe", who'd changed her name to "Trent". They tempted fate by writing "We'll Be With You" just *before* the semi-final win, and later recorded the fans singing in Stoke's Social Club.

Didn't the players record it then? Don't go there! Dudley claims that the players never sang on the record, that it was all fans and session-men. Many of the players don't remember (eg. Mike Bernard), some weren't allowed to sing (eg. Jackie Marsh, Terry Lees) and some genuinely weren't there (eg. Terry Conroy). A charade? Maybe we will never know.

As Chelsea had done their own song (Blue Is The Colour), I bet Stoke's directors were proud of the song. Despite the whole-world-and-his-dog knowing the song was being recorded, Stoke's directors miserably denied knowledge of the project and petulantly refused to fund it.

Mean old gits! Thankfully, Tony Hatch paid half with Dudley cunningly finding the other half from the club shop takings! When it sold well, making No.34 in the charts, the Stoke board (allegedly) had the nerve to pocket all the profits. Hatch didn't mind – he was on his way to being a multi-millionaire songwriter anyway (he wrote the "Neighbours" TV theme).

Was it played at Wembley? No, they played Chelsea at Wembley. Oh, sorry, er yes, The Royal Marine Band played it before the game!

Were Chelsea also played at Wembley? Yes! Chelsea had beaten Spurs to reach the final. They had already won the League Cup in 1965 – unlike Stoke, they'd actually managed to beat Leicester. They went on to win the FA Cup in 1970 and the Cup Winners Cup in 1971. With a cracking team that included Osgood, Hudson, Hollins, Webb, Cooke and Harris they were on a roll to big things.

I blame Peter Bonetti! And rightly so, but The Cat (as he was called) was still one of the best keepers in the world. But he was no Gordon Banks.

THE FINAL!

Who played for Stoke? Oh, the usual suspects:
Goalkeeper: Gordon Banks;
Back Four: Jackie Marsh, Denis Smith, Alan Bloor, Mike Pejic;
Midfield: Peter Dobing(c), Mike Bernard, George Eastham;
Strikers: Terry Conroy, John Ritchie, Jimmy Greenhoff;
Sub: John Mahoney.
If you can't repeat this team like a mantra, then learn it. One day you will be tested! And on that day you must not be caught wanting.

Did anyone turn up to watch? 97,852. It seemed like most of Stoke-on-Trent was there, a sea of red and white.

Chelsea were more used to Wembley. But it was Stoke who scored first. In only the fifth minute, the ball pinballed around the penalty area until Conroy somehow managed to head the ball beyond Bonetti for 1-0.

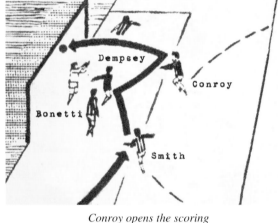

Conroy opens the scoring

I blame Peter Bonetti! And rightly so, although Conroy's header arc-ed way beyond his grasp. However, Banks pulled off some really great

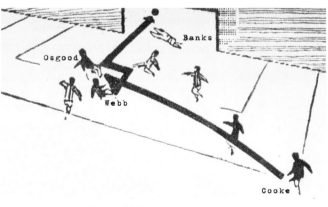

Osgood falls over and equalises

saves at the other end as Chelsea pressured for the rest of the half. Just on half-time, Peter Osgood, who'd tumbled over in the penalty area, stuck out his foot, and the ball bumbled past Banks, to make it 1-1.

Did Stoke fall apart? No, they came out fighting, and early in the second half Ritchie had a goal disallowed. But eventually they were rewarded when Bonetti palmed away a Greenhoff volley and George Eastham (36) swept in to score a rare goal to make it 2-1. He's still the oldest man to score in a Wembley final. OK, he's 73 now, but I don't think anyone older than that will score at Wembley.

I blame Peter Bonetti! And rightly so, although it was a great save from Greenhoff. Even greater was Banks' save at the other end. Bernard's back-pass in the final seconds fell to Chris Garland, but Banks rushed out to deflect the shot wide.

And that's why Stoke won? Exactly.

And that's why Mike Bernard had a daughter the following day? Er, yes. Mrs Bernard went into labour after that back-pass. The rest of us just had kittens.

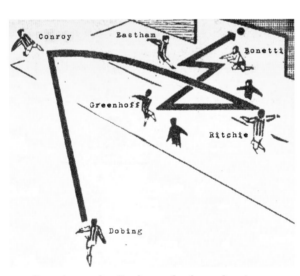

Bonetti saves, but Eastham pokes home the winner

Are you sure it was Chris Garland who received Bernard's back-pass? Denis Smith reckoned it was Tommy Baldwin. Bernard claimed it was Peter Osgood. Terry Conroy has even written that it was *Colin* Garland (the Jamaican artist). Some even think it was just a guy selling peanuts, but I've seen the clip many times, and it is surely the blonde bombshell Chris Garland (even Banksy says so).

What happened next? Well, after missing that chance, Chris Garland's career went into decline. He even started a fruit and veg business, but it just went pear-shaped.

I meant what happened next at Wembley?! Oh, right. Well, the final whistle finally went, Peter Dobing collected the League Cup, Stoke fans drowned out the National Anthem, and then there was that bus ride through the crowded streets of Stoke-on-Trent.

What happened to Mike Bernard? Even before the end of the season he was bought by Everton. He didn't want to go, but Stoke needed the money, as always.

What happened to Chelsea? Ah, now this is interesting. They didn't recover for decades. Despite being one of the hottest sides at the time, they went on to not win anything for 25 years. After losing the final against Stoke, things fell apart big time. Many players left – including Alan Hudson to Stoke – and two years later so did manager Dave Sexton. Whilst Stoke were excelling, Chelsea were relegated. Although they struggled back a couple of times, they soon went down again, almost dropping into the Third Division. They only finally returned to the top-flight for good in 1989.

If only someone famous, like Chelsea's king of Stamford Bridge Peter "Ossie" Osgood, agreed with your theory. In his autobiography, *Ossie, King Of Stamford Bridge*, Peter Osgood agrees with this theory, saying, "I suppose you could carbon-date the start of Chelsea and my own decline from that day and George Eastham's goal."

George Eastham, hero
©Philip Neill

So Chelsea's demise in the 1970s really was all Stoke's fault? Well, partly. Well, quite a bit. Actually, yes, it was all our fault. OK?

Brings tears to your eyes. Yeah, I haven't laughed so much in years.

Stoke City's1972 heroes
©Bob Bond

It was a busy couple of years, one way or the other.

STOKE CITY IN FIRST EVER FA CUP PENALTY SHOOT OUT!

Birmingham City 0 Stoke City 0 (FA Cup Final)

5th August 1972

Now I REALLY don't remember this one! You and everyone else.

Maybe the legendary Birmingham striker Trevor Francis can throw some light on the matter? Trevor was recently interviewed by The Independent newspaper. When asked what he remembered of the game, he replied that he had absolutely no recollection of it whatsoever.

Was it that dull? No, it was far worse than that. It sent 24,000 fans into a coma. Many never recovered, suffering decades of turning up and supporting Birmingham in a dazed and confused state.

OK, OK. Was it one of these 3rd/4th playoff games? Absolutely. In its third year and still going strong. The following year Wolves won at Arsenal, which went off OK, but the year after that a pathetic 4000 turned out to see Burnley win at Leicester.

Nothing is as it seems in Birmingham

A pathetic 4000 isn't bad for a Leicester v Burnley game! Yes, it is. Anyway, that was it, as far as the FA were concerned. The experiment was over – trust Burnley to ruin it for everyone else - and the $3^{rd}/4^{th}$ playoff was canned after only 5 years, and quite rightly so.

Why was it played in August? As Stoke had so many cup runs in 1972, ending up playing 67 games in total, they had a huge backlog of league games. This playoff was scheduled for the evening before the cup-final, but Stoke had to play West Brom that night. Three days later they were at Newcastle United. It was never going to happen.

The usual suspects

I bet the guys at Selhurst Park weren't pleased! They were probably over-the-moon not to have to host the game. Whereas only 5,000 turned up there to see Stoke v Everton the previous season, this time the game was played at Birmingham's St Andrews ground, attracting nearly 5 times as many fans.

Not bad for what effectively was a pre-season friendly.

So how did Stoke and Birmingham end up here? Well, they both made the FA Cup semi-finals. Stoke got there by firstly beating off Chesterfield. This should have been an easy home game against a third division team, but Stoke struggled to a 2-1 win, with goals from Conroy and Dobing. In the next round, City were cruising to a 2-0 win at Tranmere, but the Rovers almost pinched it in the last 10 minutes – Stoke hung on for 2-2. Stoke beat 10-men Tranmere 2-0 in the replay. Second division Hull were then dispensed with by 4-1.

Anyone good in the Quarter Final? Bloomin' Manchester United again! It had taken them 3 games to beat them in the League Cup a few months before. Despite both sides at full strength – Bobby Charlton, George Best, Denis Law etc – it ended 1-1, with Greenhoff putting in the rebound off Alec Stepney, but Best poking in a late equaliser.

Back to the Victoria Ground? Absolutely. Best scored first this time - a cracker on 70 minutes - with Denis Smith heading the equaliser four minutes later. In extra time, Conroy struck the winner, and United's demise at the hands of Stoke City continued.

I'm still laughing from last time. And it's just as funny this time. Soon United were mixing with the likes of Oxford, York and Orient, whilst Stoke were at the top of the League above Arsenal and Liverpool. Funny old world.

Anyone good in the Semi Final? Nope, boring boring Arsenal, again. Time for revenge for last year!

REVENGE FOR LAST YEAR!
STOKE CITY V ARSENAL

Did we get revenge? Sort of.

Sort of??! Well, in an exciting match at Villa Park, Arsenal went one up after the break, but Smith forced an own-goal off Simpson to level it at 1-1. Another injured keeper - this time Bob Wilson and his knee, after Denis Smith gently knocks him off-balance (yeah, right!) - but Stoke can't get a winner past stand-in keeper John Radford. So, it's off to Goodison Park.

Goodison Park? I have a bad feeling about this. And so you should. However, Stoke had a dream start when Frank McLintock took out Jimmy Greenhoff.

Let someone else . . .

do the driving

Better go by

JPMT

THE POTTERIES MOTOR TRACTION CO. LTD.,
Head Office — Woodhouse St. Stoke-on-Trent.
Telephone 48811

Must have been a strange dream. It was. Greenhoff scored from the subsequent penalty after 20 minutes. 1-0.

Seven luxury PMT coaches were stoned at Goodison Park that day. In the pictures above only the driver was stoned.

Did the dream become a nightmare? 'Fraid so. In the second half, Dobing was alleged to have pushed little George Armstrong in the back in an off-the-ball incident. Armstrong went down in a heap, but Dobing still claims he never touched him. Even Arsenal were bewildered to find themselves with a penalty. Charlie George stepped up, said thanks very much, and it was 1-1.

Were there ghosts in this nightmare. 'Fraid so. 15 minutes from the end, Charlie George was through, but 20,000 miles offside. The linesman failed to flag as he saw a ghostly figure in white on the far side, which he assumed was a Stoke defender as Stoke were playing in white that night, and all their defenders looked pretty ghastly.

Have you seen this man?!

Ghostly!! Oh sorry, I mean *ghostly*, not ghastly. Anyway, it turned out it was an Everton programme/ice-cream/peanut seller on the far side of the pitch who was also dressed in white. In the meantime, Charlie George pulled the ball back for Radford to score the winner, and Stoke were out. Ludicrous. You just could'ner make it up.

What happened to the peanut seller? Intriguing. Turns out there were no peanuts on sale that night. And who sells ice-cream on a late mid-April night? And everyone knows programme sellers give up as soon as the match starts. That man – if he was a man – has never …. been seen ….again (and a lot of Stokies have been wanting a word with him for decades). Maybe…he was never there!

What did linesman Bob Matthewson have to say for himself? "I'm completely blind. I told them I wasn't up for the job, but they took my white stick away and gave me a flag to hold."

And what did linesman Bob Matthewson *really* have to say for himself? He said, he got it wrong and was sorry. Mind you, it was Denis Smith who was asking him, and you don't say no to Denis.

And what did Tony Waddington say? "Don't go into the dressing room yet. The boys are a bit violent at the moment."

What happened to Arsenal? It's funny you should ask. They lost the FA Cup final to Leeds (yawn), lost another cup final several years later to Ipswich, didn't win anything for years, etc etc. The double winning side was broken up, and the club went through a selection of hapless managers. Read Nick Hornby's *Fever Pitch* for the misery and dejection they and their supporters suffered for decades. It will really cheer you up.

And Stoke were responsible for this? Excellent, makes you proud!
Actually, this time Stoke can't take all of the blame. The fact is they'd signed Alan Ball several months before, and well, need we say more.

So Stoke can be blamed/credited for the demise of Man Utd and Chelsea, but Alan Ball takes the biscuit for Arsenal? That's the way the cookie crumbles.

And this all leads untidily to the Birmingham City 3rd/4th playoff final? As it was played at the start of the following season, Stoke cheated dreadfully by giving debuts to two new signings, Jimmy Robertson and a famous World Cup hat-trick bloke called Geoff Hurst, whom Waddington had pinched from West Ham.

Why was that cheating?
Neither should have been eligible to play as they were cup-tied to other clubs,

Alan Ball was so small that they used to keep him in a match-box

meaning that they played for two different clubs in the same FA Cup competition. However, Birmingham cheated too, playing new signings Bobby Hope and Tony Want. They also fielded top strikers Trevor Francis, Bob Latchworth, Bob Hatton and one Gordon Taylor (now head of the PFA).

With these sort of players it should have been a cracker! It was a bore-fest, with snoring heard from the terraces during extra-time. Ritchie and Hurst missed easy chances, Latchworth and Smith cancelled each other out at the other end, but goalie John Farmer – deputising for injured Banks – was man of the match.

But apart from the cheating, was there at least one exciting and historical moment? Indeed. The first ever FA Cup penalty shootout. Birmingham won it by 4-3 when Peter Dobing's shot was saved. Farmer was even booked for twice moving before the ball was kicked, which was a bit harsh for a pre-season game. But the trip to St Andrews wasn't all for nothing. The players all received tankards, which at least had a more practical use than medals.

Are you being ironic here? I'm sure am. The tankards were complete tack.

Penalty save! Peter Dobing immortalised in cartoon form.
©Bob Bond

So, did this lead to more cup success for Stoke City? It sure did!

So, did this lead to more FA Cup success for Stoke City? Ah, no. Sorry. Stoke haven't even made the 6th round since. In fact, Stoke are the 9th worst league team when it comes to the FA Cup. However, I think it's going to change …soon! Oh, no, hang on, I've just heard on the radio that they've just gone out of the cup to Hartlepool United. Knickers! Forget the whole thing.

STOKE SCRUB AJAX TO A 0-0 DRAW!

Ajax 0 Stoke City 0 (UEFA Cup)

2nd October 1974

We shall fight them on the beaches! And what relevance is this again?

Er, nothing. So, why were Stoke in Europe again? If you exclude playing Motherwell in The Texaco Cup, then 1972 was Stoke's first real jaunt into European football proper. They entered the UEFA Cup as winners of the League Cup.

So suddenly, they were amongst the big boys! Who did they get to play? Real Madrid? Bayern Munich? Barcelona? Er, no. It was a German side called Kaiserslautern.

Kaiserslautern? Where the hell's that?
Exactly. It's south-west Germany, near the French and Swiss borders - Steve McQueen probably went past it on his motorbike. Chelsea's Michael Ballack and Fulham's Mark Schwarzer played there briefly in the mid-1990s.

But were they any good? They had been good in the 1950s, but were going into a decline. They pompously turned up at The Victoria Ground, demanded that they be allowed to train on the pitch, insisted that Stoke play in their away strip, and were soundly beaten by 3-1, with second half goals from Conroy, Hurst and Ritchie, although they should have scored more. However, Kaiserslautern's late away goal was crucial to them.

Did it all go wrong for Stoke in the return leg? You can say that again.

Did it all go wrong for Stoke in the return leg? Yes! Firstly, although Stoke remembered to fly out numerous directors and VIPs, they forgot the first-team coach, the fuming Alan A'Court. He was flown out late on a charter flight with some fans, and arrived just before the game. Then the Germans wouldn't let Stoke have their dressing-room.

Why not? Get this: they claimed that there was a women's match on before the main game, and that the girls were using the away dressing-room.

And this was a problem?? Exactly, I'd have just said, "OK, we'll share it then!" But Tony Waddington was a gentleman, and had the players changing in a prefab hut with a

England's Alan A'Court (left) slides in to score at Wembley

team-talk in the hotel lounge. Mind you, no one heard him anyway - his pre-match briefing was drowned out by a pneumatic drill a few yards away.

Anything else? Stoke were without Gordon Banks (shoulder strain), and John Ritchie was left on the bench as the team attempted to defend a 3-1 lead. They failed.

How bad? One down on 20 minutes. The second goal was on the stroke of half-time, and although the linesman flagged it offside, the Polish referee ignored him. By the time it reached the hour-mark, it was 0-3 and probably too late for John Ritchie to make a difference, but Waddington sent him on anyway.

Where was he sitting? You don't half ask some strange questions. Bizarrely the away bench was positioned behind the goal at the far end, with the home bench behind the nearside goal, beside the players' tunnel. John Ritchie came on from the away bench, and brushed against their centre-half, who'd positioned himself in Ritchie's way to give him a shove as he passed. As if shot by a poacher, the centre-half threw himself to the ground, and the immediately red-carded Ritchie just kept on jogging past the home bench into the tunnel. He'd been on the pitch about 30 seconds, and all he'd done was run from one end of the pitch to the other end and then disappeared!

Time to go home? Definitely. Kaiserslautern scored a fourth, and were taken off Stoke's Christmas card list. For their penance they spent nearly 20 years in the doldrums before they won anything again. Bit like Arsenal. Only with less class.

The curse of Stoke City had struck again? No, Kaiser were just crap.

Did Gordon Banks play again? He played 4 more games before being badly injured in a car-crash, losing the sight in one eye. Although he had already been playing first-team football for 14 years, it was clear he had several years at the top left, sadly stolen from him.

Did he retire? No, but he was reduced to working in the colonies.

Now stop being snobbish. The standard was pretty good out there. OK, I'll give you that, and moreover, Banksy became USA's Goalkeeper Of The Year!

So how did Stoke end up playing Ajax? By finishing fifth in the league. They'd spent most of the season fighting relegation. In fact they'd spent most of the last decade fighting relegation. But then in January 1974 they signed someone who would change all that. His name was Alan Hudson.

One day this kid would grow up to be Big John Ritchie

Did he make any difference? Well, Stoke were quite proud that they'd made it as high as 17th position by mid-January. But with Hudson they then beat Liverpool 1-0, Chelsea 1-0 (twice), and Manchester United 1-0. Best of all Stoke came from 0-2 down to beat soon-to-be-champions Leeds United by 3-2, ending the Leeds 29 game unbeaten run. With three wins at the end of the season they staggered up to 5th position on the last day, pushing Burnley out of a UEFA spot.

Should we feel sorry for Burnley? No. They would later knock us out of the cup. However, the curse of Stoke City struck them hardest. After being denied a chance in Europe by Stoke, they were relegated from the top-flight and have only just clawed their way back after 33 years! Sorry, guys. No hard feelings, eh?

Anyway, weren't we talking about Ajax, the bath and floor cleaner? No, we're talking about Ajax of Amsterdam. In the early 1970s they were full of bull; ie. formidabull, invincibull and unstoppabull.

How formidable, invincible and unstoppable were they? Between 1970 and 1973 they won the Dutch league 3 times out of 4, they won the Dutch Cup 3 times in a row, and they won the European Cup 3 times in a row. They invented a new style of play called "Total Football"; their nickname was "The Sons of Gods"; and their squad was called the "Twelve Apostles".

Blasphemy!!! Normally I'd agree. But the 12 players included such stars as Johan Cruyff, Rudi Krol and Johnny Rep.

What?? Johnny Depp – star of Pirates Of The Caribbean - played for Ajax??! No, Johnny *Rep*, scorer of the winning goal in the 1973 European Cup final against Juventus.

So he doesn't have a chocolate factory? No, he doesn't. This was Johnny *Rep*, junior member of the "Twelve Apostles".

Hang on, if Ajax were so formid-vincible, what were they doing slumming it in the UEFA Cup? In 1973, they sold Cruyff to Barcelona, and the side started to break up. In 1974 they failed to win anything. And by September they found themselves at the Victoria Ground, with only 5 remaining apostles. There was also the hangover of Holland losing the World Cup final to West Germany a few weeks earlier. And the knowledge that the UEFA Cup was not going to be easy: the likes of Juventus and Inter Milan were also in the competition.

So, who did Stoke have to counter the likes of Krol and Rep? Stoke played Alan Hudson, although still dazed from a car-crash several days before. They were also without Ritchie (suspended) and Hurst (bereavement). However, they did still have the likes of Greenhoff, Conroy, Pejic, Denis Smith and new signing Geoff Salmons.

How did they match up? Ajax were given too much space in the middle, and Stoke couldn't get the ball off them. Krol blasted home before half time for a 0-1 lead. Then Jimmy Robertson came on in the second half, and soon Smith was lunging in the equaliser (he needed three stitches). 1-1 against Ajax was pretty impressive, but getting a result at Amsterdam's Olympic stadium would be a different matter.

Was it a different matter? Back came Hudson and Hurst, fit and able. Up stepped Salmons and Pejic to terrorise their defence. And then there was Greenhoff, aided by Sean Haslegrave and Conroy, stretching Piet Schrijvers in goal. No John Ritchie, though – his career had been ended with a broken leg at Ipswich.

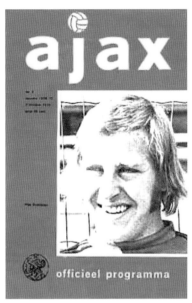

What about Denis Smith? Oh, he was in stitches again. Then he needed two more in his knee early in the game. No real surprise there.

Did anyone think Stoke had a chance in Amsterdam? Everyone had written them off, but it was Stoke who had the better chances. After John Farmer had made a few fine saves for Stoke, Ajax found themselves desperately defending their away goal, as Stoke realised that one goal could win it for them. Chances fell to Greenhoff, Conroy, Haslegrave, and even super-sub Robertson nearly clinched it in the last few minutes, with his shot flying wide via the goalie's outstretched left boot.

Well, it looks like a wig to me

But Ajax survived? Shell-shocked and under siege, they were glad to hear the final whistle. 0-0, and through on the away goals rule.

Did Ajax suffer the Stoke City curse? Yes, they went back to cleaning baths and floors. Their "Total Football" had turned into "total crap football" after facing The Potters, and they took several years to return to domestic success. But it was decades before they returned to European success though, and finally in the 1990s Ajax again won every competition worth winning (except the Autoglass Trophy).

Did John Farmer play again? Several games later John was replaced by new signing Peter Shilton, and John never played for Stoke again, preferring instead to retire at only 27. The irony was that John had pleaded to be released by Stoke when he was Gordon Banks' understudy, but they wouldn't let him go.

And who did Stoke play next in Europe? That was it, as far as major competitions were concerned.

How can this be? 1974/75 was one of their best ever seasons? That is correct. They even spent a few weeks top of the league, but ended 5th again, only 4 points off Derby County, who won the championship with only 21 wins out of 42 games. But the UEFA Cup, being the replacement for the Inter-Cities Fairs Cup, still had the loony one-club-per-city rule, although by now it was only applied in England. As Liverpool had qualified for the UEFA Cup by finishing 2nd, Everton were excluded by the rule, even though they'd finished 4th. So they belly-ached to UEFA. But as Waddington pointed out, Everton had known the rule for the whole of the season, and anyway, the Football League backed Stoke. "Changing it now would be farcical," he added.

Somewhere in this picture is Denis Smith (horizontal). Is it any wonder that he was always broken.

So Stoke should have qualified? Yes, only Everton appealed and won, and the rule was scrapped, leaving Stoke out in the cold. Just like the man said: farcical.

But, sweet revenge for Everton after losing that 3rd/4th playoff. True, but then one more point in the league would have seen Stoke finish above Everton anyway.

Still, Stoke had a superb squad. Yes, it featured Denis Smith (broken leg), Jimmy Robertson (broken leg), Mike Pejic (broken leg), John Ritchie (broken leg), Jimmy Greenhoff (broken nose), Terry Conroy (broken cartilage), and Alan Hudson (broken car).

But at least Stoke's future looked secure. Yep, as safe as houses, and as secure as, well, a stadium roof.

Three years later...

STOKE IN RECURRING NON-LEAGUE NIGHTMARE!

Stoke City 2 Blyth Spartans 3
(FA Cup 4th Round)

6th February 1978

What the hell had happened in just three years? Well, it's a funny thing, really: Stoke City had entered the world of … Narnia!

Er, right. In what way? The great Aslan, who had inspired all creatures great and small, had disappeared; all his loyal followers were scattered to the four corners of the kingdom; and the evil white witch had arrived to make an enchantment so that it was always winter but never Christmas.

OK, so that's taken care of The Lion and The Witch. What about the Wardrobe? Ah yes, the wardrobe. Yeah, I'm not sure where that fits in. Maybe Mike Pejic made one with all the wood he pinched from the fallen Butler Street stadium roof. Who knows.

So, who was Aslan? Tony Waddington, of course. After the club hit the financial skids (when the stand roof blew off), he was forced to sell his star players for a pittance. As the team went into free-fall, he stepped down in 1977 in disgust after 17 years in charge. The spirit of Waddington would return though like Obi-Wan Kenobi.

Funny, I don't remember Obi-Wan Kenobi in the Narnia stories. Oh sorry, that's Star Wars, isn't it? Damn, and I was going to have Tony Waddington as a Jedi Knight. That wouldn't quite work in Narnia.

So what four corners did his followers get scattered? Alan Hudson went to Arsenal, Jimmy Greenhoff to Manchester United, Mike Pejic to Everton and Peter Shilton to Nottingham Forest. They were replaced by the unknown and the inexperienced, and Stoke were soon relegated. After Waddington's replacement, George Eastham, had been sacked in January 1978, coach Alan A'Court took temporary charge.

So, who was Alan A'Court in this Narnia analogy? I think he was the faun, Mr Tumnus. He did his best, but got turned into stone. Metaphorically.

So where does this "winter but never Christmas" bit fit in? Oh yes. Heavy snow came down, and the season dragged to a halt for weeks. With Stoke's position in the 2nd Division looking perilous, the Blyth game came along as a litmus test to ascertain just how Stoke were coping with lower league football.

How perilous was the position? Just before the snow they could only manage to draw 1-1 at home to relegation-chasing Mansfield, with Denis Smith, now Captain Smith, getting injured…again.

Wasn't it also a Stoke-born Captain Smith who went down with the Titanic? Er, yes. Then Stoke lost 0-1 at bottom club, Burnley, dropping to a lowly 15th position. In the following *6 weeks*, Stoke only played one game due to the weather. That game... was at home to Blyth Spartans.

Not knowing which way to turn, this Captain Smith went down with the boat

What was Blyth doing here? They'd come from the land of the ice and snow, from the midnight sun where the hot springs blow…

I beg your pardon?! Well, just north of Newcastle-upon-Tyne, anyway. They'd beaten four local teams to reach the FA Cup first round, only to find themselves up against *another* non-league team, Burscough (pronounced Burs/co), winning 1-0. They then saw off 3rd Division Chesterfield by 1-0 to reach the third round. However, instead of getting Man Utd, they got yet *another* non-league team, Enfield, beating them (you guessed it) 1-0. They'd got the binary system (1-0) pretty bad, long before Tony Pulis was infected.

Did Blyth get Man Utd in the 4th round? Of course they didn't. They got 2nd Division Stoke City, away.

So, how did Stoke get to the 4th round? Stoke had prepared for the Blyth game by beating Tilbury of the Isthmian League by 4-0. Tilbury were their first non-league opposition since being beaten by Rhyl in 1926, so some improvement in 50 years.

So, did Stoke get Man Utd in the 4th round? Of course they didn't! They got Blyth Spartans, only the game was called off twice due to the weather. The draw for the next round had long since been made, and their next opponents would be Blyth's neighbours, top-flight Newcastle United (unless little Wrexham could beat them).

Were Stoke scared? Certainly not. They'd beaten Blyth before in the cup back in 1923, so Aslan's mighty army were on a roll. Sort of.

Howard Kendall kept a squirrel on his head to keep him warm.

Who did Stoke have in their, er, mighty Aslan army? Howard Kendall, the former Everton star, was settling well in midfield after being signed by Eastham, who'd also acquired veteran Liverpool defender, Alec Lindsey. Jackie Marsh, Terry Conroy and Alan Bloor were the only remaining players from the League Cup success. Smith was out injured, but long-server Alan Dodd was present-and-correct. Garth Crooks was still emerging as the star player he would later become at Spurs. And then there was Viv Busby, who knew a thing or two.

What thing-or-two did he know? Busby was playing for top-flight Newcastle the day when non-league Hereford United beat them with that Ronnie Radford screamer in 1972 (cue John Motson going berserk) – one of the upsets of the century (apart from a couple of World Wars, JFK's assassination, and Boom Bang-a-Bang winning the Eurovision Song Contest). And talking of upsets, Alan A'Court was playing for Liverpool when they were knocked out by almost fictional Worcester City, so Stoke had a wealth of experience about losing to non-league folk.

Good playing surface? Quagmire, more like. The game having been called off twice, should probably have been called off again. Many Blyth fans who'd tried to make the first two dates, were unable to get to the third, and bitterly regret it to this day.

What did they miss? In front of nearly 19,000 fans, Blyth went one up after only 11 minutes. The goal was scored (or so it was reported) by 38-year-old Terry Johnson, who poked the ball home from a corner whilst waiting for his pension to arrive. However, with the supporters right behind them (behind them in the "wielding baseball bats" sense, not in the "friendly" sense), Stoke went 2-1 up after the break, with goals from Busby and Crooks.

There, you see. What was the problem? This was the game that was to show where Stoke stood in the great order of things. Were they sleeping giants, or a club settling in to spend a generation underachieving in the lower divisions?

Would Aslan return to save them? No. Unfortunately, Stoke's defence decided things for them, by allowing a sloppy equaliser on 75 minutes, with the ball hitting both posts before Steve Carney finished the job. Then 73-year-old Terry Johnson, who was about to nod off in his favourite armchair, scored an even sloppier decider on 88 minutes.

The man who knew too much: Viv Busby. He knew how to lose to non-league people.
(©News Group Newspapers)

Bit "age-ist", all this? Not at all. Terry deservedly humbled the mighty Stoke, clutching his telegram from the Queen as he did so. That's all we really know.

Hm, if only manager Alan A'Court had written a book about his life in football, then he could have told us more. Thankfully, Alan A'Court has written a book about his life in football called *My Life In Football*, where he tells us more.

What a bit of luck! What does he say? He reckons it was all Howard Kendall's fault. Kendall had been made team captain, and thought he knew a thing or two.

Well, he did go on to win championships and cups managing Everton. Yes, but Alan A'Court was manager that day, not Kendall. A'Court reckoned aging Alec Lindsey lacked pace, particularly on that dreadful surface, so put him in midfield rather than full-back. Soon after half time, Kendall decided to switch him back, and A'Court watched in horror as Lindsey was run ragged. Stoke lost, A'Court got sacked, and Kendall flourished. Funny old world.

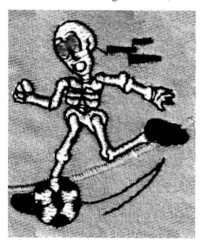

Blyth's youthful Terry Johnson scoring the winner! Actually rumours of his age were cruelly exaggerated.

Alan A'Court's post-match quote? "We played like schoolboys."

So did Blyth beat Newcastle in the fifth round? No, they never got to play their neighbours as United had got beat by 3rd Division Wrexham. Blyth took the Robins to a replay, which was hosted at St James Park in front of 42,000! They lost 1-2.

Collateral damage? By reaching a fifth round replay, Blyth went further in the FA Cup than any other non-League team had done since before the First World War (and the Eurovision Song Contest). Stoke City, on the other hand, had a big hole to dig themselves out of.

So, was that the end for Stoke? Well, it was the end for Alec Lindsey and Alan Bloor. They never played for Stoke again. But the Blyth Spartans result sent a message out to the world that Stoke were no longer the great side they had been.

Proof? The next time Stoke played non-league opposition in the cup, it was Telford United. Stoke had been relegated to the 3rd Division under Alan Ball.

Not Alan Ball?!?!! Yes, get over it. If it makes you feel better, he was probably Reepicheep in Narnia, the incredibly annoying fighting mouse with the high-pitched voice.

But Stoke didn't lose, did they? True. A 0-0 draw away was followed by a tight 1-0 win at home, the first time Stoke had been shown live on TV.

So? The following season, with Lou Macari in charge, and Stoke fighting for promotion to the 2nd Division, Telford took them to a replay after a 0-0 draw at the Victoria Ground, and beat Stoke 1-2

And your point? The Telford games barely registered on the radar.

Aslan the lion used radar??!! No, what I mean is that when Stoke lost to Blyth Spartans, the world sat up and took notice. People can even remember where they were. But when they lost to Telford, a few people shrugged their shoulders, turned off their radar machines and went home. It showed just how unimportant Stoke had become. But under Macari (Prince Caspian) that was all going to change.

Can I mention Nuneaton Borough now? A case in point. In the year 2000 under Gudjon Thordarson (Puddleglum in Narnia) (Now, doesn't that name fit?!), Stoke were in the 3rd Division again (although it was called Div 2 by now). Up stepped conference side Nuneaton Borough in the FA Cup 1st round, and forced a 0-0 draw at the Victoria Ground. Stoke went down 0-1 in the replay, and nobody batted an eyelid.

Why's that? Because they'd got their eyes shut. It was just too awful to watch.

Captain Smith – often in a worse state than the pitch

I've just got one more question: why did Stoke play in yellow and blue that night against Blyth? Yeah, and who shot JFK? Where is Lord Lucan? What happened to the Marie Celeste? Just another complete mystery. One theory put forward: the game was being televised, and their strips would have looked too similar on black and white TV? Anything's possible.

How did The Sentinel report it? "A night Stoke City will want to forget – and never will." Er, yeah, that makes a lot of sense.

STOKE REIGNING CHAMPIONS!

Stoke City 2 Hull City 0 (Watney Cup Final)

18th August 1973

I know that one day when I'm old and grey, and can't get out much, my grandchildren will come running in from playing on the internet (or whatever they'll have then) shouting, "Grandad, Zak says that Stoke City once won a thing called The What-knee Cup. But Peaches says he's making it up. Who's right. Grandad?" And what will you tell them?

I'll tell them to pop next door, prod you in your wheel chair, and to ask you! Well, if you go to the Stoke City website, it does name the Watney Cup as the seventh most important trophy that they've won, just above the Football Alliance League Champions of 1891.

Now that's what I call a big cup

So, what on earth was the Watney Cup? It was an August-based pre-season competition that ran for 4 years (1970-73). It was competed for by the two top scorers in each of the four divisions of the Football League (who hadn't got promotion or weren't in a European competition or had anything better to do). It featured an experimental offside rule (ie. just in the penalty area), was the first British tournament to use penalty shoot-outs to decide games, and it was shown live on TV. It was also a forerunner for all the later sponsor deals in football; it was actually called The Watney Mann Invitation Cup. It really was up itself.

It was a disgusting use of alcohol sponsorship in football; almost as bad as betting! Dreadful, I agree. A plague of locusts on us all!

But Stoke won it, so we don't care. Yeah, I'll drink to that! Although Watney's Pale Ale was a bit grim. Stoke got to the final by winning 1-0 at Plymouth with a Geoff Hurst goal. Then Hurst, Pejic, Conroy and Greenhoff saw off Bristol City 4-1.

That simple, eh? How did the final go? At the Victoria Ground, 18,159 watched Stoke beat 2nd Division Hull City by 2-0, Greenhoff scoring both.

How did the Sentinel describe all this? "Unmemorable."

Well, who won it next? Nobody. It was cancelled after that.

So, Stoke are the reigning Watney Cup champions?! Sure are.

Have we still got the trophy?! It's actually locked up at Derby County (the first winners of the cup). They pinched it to fill their meagre trophy cabinet.

So, Stoke really do have the kiss of death? Stoke had seen off the FA Cup 3rd/4th Playoff Final, and now the Watney Cup. What else did they scupper?

The Texaco Cup

What about the Texaco Cup? Oh yes, they saw that one off as well. Sponsored by the Texaco petrol company, it was supposed to feature top clubs from England, Scotland and Ireland …who'd failed to win anything or get into Europe.

So which top Scottish/Irish team did Stoke play? Birmingham City.

Oh dear, they don't sound very Gaelic. And you're surprised *why*?! C'mon, the Texaco Cup looked good on paper, but football is played on grass.

Are you sure? Actually, it didn't even look that good on paper, now you come to mention it. The competition started in 1970/71, but by the time Stoke met Birmingham in 1973, the cup was already going to the dogs. The English clubs dominated and the Irish teams had to pull out, plus attendances were meagre as the competition seemed pointless to fans once the Scots were beaten.

But thankfully Stoke's game with Birmingham was a high-scoring thriller? Dream on. After two 0-0 draws, Stoke were beaten by Birmingham on penalties. *Again.* The Sentinel described it as "depressing" and a "pathetic failure". The most exciting thing to happen was the game being stopped by a small dog "romping" around the pitch. Oh, and Birmingham had to play their 5th choice goalkeeper who really was called Ritchie Blackmore. Despite him saving penalties from Marsh and Smith, he never played again.

But surely Stoke weren't the only reason for the decline of the Texaco Cup. I think the oil crisis had something to do with it too. A year later, Texaco pulled out, and that was that. The cup was revived as the Anglo-Scottish Cup, but it was soon populated by lower division clubs. The last two winners were St Mirren (the only Scottish winners) in 1980 and Chesterfield in 1981.

Chesterfield?! What, 3rd Division Chesterfield?! Interestingly, Chesterfield knocked out a full strength Glasgow Rangers in the quarter finals, which showed just how daft the competition had become. The following season Chesterfield were relegated to the 4th Division. Dunno what happened to Glasgow Rangers – Scottish football and all that.

BIZARRE CLUB SHIRTS

CHESTERFIELD

Thankfully the Chesterfield players didn't wear these shirts
©*Philip Neill*

So Stoke never even scored a goal in the Texaco Cup?! Untrue! When the Texaco Cup started in 1970 it was actually called the International League Board Competition (catchy title or what?!). However, it was referred to in the press as The British Isles Cup. Texaco came in late to sponsor it, and it was then called "The Texaco sponsored British Cup".

And then it became the Texaco Cup? No, it became the Texaco International League Competition. Ugh!

And your point? Before it was really the Texaco Cup, Stoke were in the very first round. They lost 0-1 at Motherwell (who really were Scottish, and not from Birmingham afterall), then won 2-1 at home.

And they lost the subsequent penalty shoot-out? You guessed it. Stoke lost 3-4. Revenge was sweet the following season when they beat Motherwell 1-0 and 4-1. But the eventual winners Derby County beat Stoke 2-3 and 2-2 in the next round. This was just about acceptable as Brian Clough's Derby were League Champions that year.

But it slipped a long way to end up in Chesterfield by 1981! And the trophy is still there today. By then nobody else wanted it. Even Derby.

The Anglo-Italian Cup

Did Stoke also ruin the Anglo-Italian Cup. But of course. They were hammering nails into its coffin for years until it died. However, it was Port Vale who popped up to finally knacker it.

What the hell was it? It was originally a 1960s amateur competition between English and Italian non-league clubs. However, when Swindon won the League Cup in 1969 and were barred from entering the Inter-Cities Fairs Cup (the old UEFA Cup) for being a 3rd Division side, the organisers saw their opportunity to launch the competition with league clubs. It was designed to improve relations between the English and Italian leagues in the 1970s.

And did it? Hm, let me see: In the first final, Swindon went 3-0 up in Napoli, resulting in pitch invasions, bottle and rock throwing etc until the match was abandoned.

How did Stoke get involved? Well, with all this pitch invading, bottle and rock throwing etc, Stoke thought, "Hello, this sounds interesting. Give us some of that!"

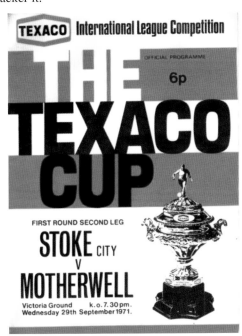

TEXACO International League Competition

6p

THE TEXACO CUP

FIRST ROUND SECOND LEG

STOKE CITY
V
MOTHERWELL

Victoria Ground   k.o.7.30pm.
Wednesday 29th September 1971.

See! It really was called the Texaco International League Competition. You think I just make this stuff up, don't you. Anyway, you can see why Derby didn't want the trophy. By the way, Texaco is now called Chevron, which isn't very interesting..

But wasn't the idea to <u>not</u> have top-flight clubs. Er, yes. The cup was for the Swindons of this world. However, after Swindon had won in 1970, all the other English entrants in 1971 were top flight. It was called cheating.

Chapter 7 – Those other cups

Did it work? Stoke won two games (Verona (h) 2-0 and AS Roma (a) 1-0) and drew two. But it was the number of goals scored that mattered, and Stoke went out, because they didn't cheat enough and score lots of goals. The following season, with more cheating going on, they won two (beating Cantanzaro 3-0 and 2-0) but lost twice to AS Roma. Somehow this resulted in Stoke finishing bottom of the "Anglo-league", thus resulting in them being eliminated, which made them realise what a waste of time it was.

But did Stoke see the cup off? Sure did. It was stopped the following year before someone got hurt. It went back to amateur clubs, before being revived in 1992 to see if there was any more mileage in crowd disturbances.

I'll bet Stoke were invited again. It couldn't be avoided, I'm afraid.

So which exotic Italian club did Stoke get to play? Birmingham City.

Oh dear, they don't sound very Italian. And you're surprised again, *why*? After beating Birmingham (2-0), and drawing 3-3 with that other exotic Italian club, Wolverhampton Wanderers, Stoke proceeded to lose to those well-known West Midlands sides, Padova (0-3) and Pescara (1-2).

Oh dear, they don't sound very West Midland. For some reason Stoke fought on. The following season saw them coast past the Italian teams, only to confront Notts County in the area final. County were bottom of the league at the time.

Penalty shoot-out defeat? Is it that obvious? After two 0-0 draws, the matter was settled on penalties, 2-3 in favour of Notts. This competition had to die!

And did it? The final season saw Stoke draw three times. When it came to their fourth and last game away to Reggiana, the game was cancelled as the pitch was flooded. Neither club would qualify anyway, so the game was just conveniently forgotten! Port Vale stumbled into the final, and were soundly beaten 5-2 by Genoa. As if this wasn't ridiculous enough, Italian tempers had risen up in the earlier rounds, although it was Birmingham City who'd somehow managed to start a massive brawl. Subsequently, someone thankfully called time on this chaos, and the cup was no more.

Did Lou Macari suggest anything sensible? He said, what about replacing it with an Anglo-Scottish Cup?! Yes, very funny, Lou.

The Full Members Simod Zenith Data Systems Cup

Any other silly competitions that Stoke ruined? What about the Full Members Cup, alias The Simod Cup, alias The Zenith Data Systems Cup.

Let me guess. It was for clubs who had failed to get into Europe, or promoted, or weren't any good, but were up for a punch-up? Sad, but so nearly true. After the Heysel Stadium disaster in 1985, English clubs and their fans were banned from European football for several years. So some idiot (probably the Football League) came up with the Full Members Cup for clubs in the top two divisions (only the top two divisions were "FULL members" of the Football League. Geddit?).

But not the top clubs? Hell, no. It was too common for them. The top 6 teams in the 1st Division played in the *Super Cup* – what a great name!

Oh, how super-dooper! That sounds so grand! The *Super Cup* was such a disaster that the final had to be played 4 months late. Liverpool's Ian Rush was supposed to be so under-whelmed by it that he gave away the trophy to some passing ball boys, and it was never seen again. Anyway, that was the *Super Cup* – still a great name – played by the clubs too posh to enter the Full Members Cup.

Oh yes, the Full Members Cup. Is it just me, or does it sound rude to you? It is a bit of a mouthful.

The Super Cup.
It was in yellow.

Anyway, moving on, how did Stoke do, seeing they were a mid-table 2nd Division team by this time? Well, they managed to beat 1st Division Coventry City 3-0 in their first game in 1985. Then in 1987 they thrashed 1st Division Portsmouth 3-0 and Sheffield Wednesday 1-0. They even won a penalty shoot-out at Leicester City by 5-3, with even Lee Dixon putting one away.

Sounds like this was the competition for Stoke! It certainly corrects the myth that when Stoke were in the lower divisions they couldn't beat top-flight clubs. Also proves that Stoke could win at penalties.

But somehow I suspect you're not really impressed, are you? Hardly. Only 3,200 fans turned up for the Portsmouth game at Fratton Park. After beating decent teams, Stoke would go out to clubs like Oxford and Luton (then lowly

1st Division clubs, now non-league clubs). They lost their last game 5-4 on penalties to Leeds in 1989. And after that, they didn't even enter at all.

Now that is brilliant. I'm really impressed. At last a club smart enough to **stand up and say, "This is a useless, stupid, moronic load of crud, with a pathetic little trophy not worthy enough to give away to a ball-boy. You can shove your cup where the sun don't shine, coz we're not entering it anymore!!!" Is that what happened?** Not exactly. Stoke got relegated to the 3rd Division, and so weren't eligible to enter anymore.

Doesn't sound so impressive when you put it like that. By the time they got promoted again, clubs were back in Europe, and the cup was in the bin (also known as Nottingham Forest, who were the last winners).

So, finally, who were Simod, and what was a Zenith Data System? Well, a Simod was a very small group of monks, too small to live in a monastery; and a Zenith Data System was a device to analyse flying insects in space.

And who were they really? Sorry. Simod were an obscure Italian sports shoe manufacturer. They thought sponsoring an English football cup would raise their profile. How dumb can you get? Zenith Data Systems were very early pioneers of laptops, in the 1980s.

Aren't they better known for allegedly promising *free* Windows upgrades to the US Air Force? Let's just say that it was no surprise when they were gobbled up by Packard Bell & NEC.

The DeLorean Cup – open to clubs who'd failed to get into Europe, and were close to bankruptcy. It would have been seriously over-subscribed.

Who would have been in line to take over the sponsorship of the cup after 1992? If the cup had continued, they had a choice of Ratners Jewellery, Barings Bank, or DeLorean cars.

Are you suggesting that there could have been a DeLorean Cup?! Now that *would* have been worth winning!

STOKE'S WINNING WEMBLEY SREAK CONTINUES!

Stoke City 1 Stockport County 0 (Autoglass Trophy Final)

16th May 1992

Wow! Stoke were back with a vengeance! If you say so.

Back on top! Back at Wembley! Back on…TV? Yeah, I suppose.

What is the matter with you?! Well, do you know anything about the Autoglass Trophy?

Was it made of glass? No, it wasn't! It was made by some brainless nerds who thought clubs in the lower divisions didn't have enough to do, thank-you-very-much.

Did lower division sides have enough to do? Of course they did. They had 46 league games to prove to supporters that they were worth supporting for a few years more. They had 2 or 3 cup games which they prayed would lead to a glamour tie at a top Premier League side, but would usually result in them getting beat at home to non-league teams like Chasetown or Canvey Island. If things were really bad, they'd find themselves suckered into playing in some stupid Anglo-Belgium competition where they'd get to play a famous Belgian side like Peterborough United.

But surely Stoke took the Autoglass seriously? When Stoke had been in the old 2nd Division in the 1980s, they naturally could afford to look down on it…that is until they got relegated in 1990. Then they discovered the full horror of the thing.

How horror-full was it? As one of the bigger lower division clubs, Stoke were expected to win the competition, without looking like they were trying to win the competition. Thankfully, they managed to achieve this with some dignity. Bear in mind that there were other sleeping giants in the 3rd Division, such as Birmingham, Reading, Wigan, Bolton, Fulham, Hull, and WBA.

Harry Redknapp would have been nothing without his friend and mentor, Tony Pulis (top)

Where did this competition come from? From Mars, probably. It was created in 1983, as The Associate Members Cup (as it was for lower division clubs who were only second-rate "associate" members of the Football League). This was 2 years before the creation of The *Full* Members Cup.

Well, I don't remember it. That's because it was also called The Freight Rover Trophy, The Sherpa Van Trophy, and The Leyland DAF Cup.

Wow, all of those! Well, then... Then it became The Autoglass Trophy, the Auto Windscreens Shield, and The LDV Vans Trophy..

So how did Stoke do in...? Then it went on to be The Football League Trophy, which is its true un-sponsored name (like when LDV Vans dropped out, leaving no prize money?). And finally it's become The Johnstone's Paint Trophy, or the JPT, or even the Paint Pot Trophy, as it is sometimes known. Next year it could be the Kit-Kat Cup or even the Haemorrhoid Ointment Trophy.

Was it easy to apply? It didn't exclude teams who had qualified for Europe, or clubs whose supporters couldn't organise a punch up. In fact the main problem for the competition was getting the supporters along at all. Clubs like Nottingham Forest could only attract about 2000 people to games (a record low for them), but the lowest was Chester who could only find 409 able-minded people to pay to see this tosh.

Was it a farce? Not totally. Bournemouth were the first winners of the Associate Members Cup, in Harry Redknapp's first season as a manager in 1984. However, the final was supposed to be at Wembley, but in that first year the pitch was trashed by The Horse Of The Year show. So they played it at Hull. So, yes, I suppose it was a farce.

Do the numbers add up? No, and that's another thing you should think of when you set up these cup competitions.

How do you mean? The lower divisions are made up of 48 clubs. To have a successful cup competition, you have to whittle them down to 32, or increase them to 64 (or you'll end up with a last-12 rather than a last-16 in the quarter finals). So occasionally they've asked some non-league clubs to join in; and the rest of the time they give some clubs a bye in the first round.

So how did Stoke do? Under Alan Ball, they lost to Mansfield in their first attempt, in front of a crowd of 1,600. So, not a good start. However, the following season saw Lou Macari in charge. Lou had won it the previous season (as the Leyland DAF Cup) whilst being manager of Birmingham, so he knew the importance of it – a real morale boost if you can get to Wembley, that can act as a springboard to other successes.

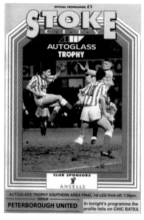

Did they get anyone interesting to play? Don't be daft. Firstly, they beat Walsall 2-0, then Lou's old club Birmingham 3-1. Then they saw off Cardiff 3-0, and then Walsall again 3-1.

A thriller!

What, they knocked Walsall out twice? Told you it was a farce. Now, this part is complicated, so listen carefully: For this tournament the country was split in two, with the winner of the North games playing the winner of The South games at Wembley. However, the first round was made up of two games in a mini-league of three teams – in this case Stoke, Walsall and Birmingham were in The South Group 5. Yes, Stoke was in The South. Walsall and Stoke got through, so they ended up playing each other later.

Well, it is grim up North. Anyway, after that it was Orient (1-0) in the quarter finals, and then Peterborough in the semis. Fans were treated to a thriller at The Victoria Ground. Biggins put Stoke 2-0 up in the first 5 minutes, but 55 minutes later it was 2-3, with Overson mistakenly slicing in their third. Finally,

Lee Sandford headed in the equaliser for 3-3. In the second leg, Paul Ware's second-half free kick won the game 1-0, and Stoke were through to the final at Wembley against Stockport County.

So, Stoke were in the South, Stockport were in The North, and the final was in London? Well, it's a day out at Wembley, and it's live on TV. What more can you ask? And it was a chance for Stoke to get revenge on Stockport knocking them out of the playoffs.

So, who was in Stoke's team? Macari had two big centre backs, Vince Overson and Ian Cranson. They had to deal with Stockport's 6ft 7in of Kevin Francis. Up front were the killer duo, Mark Stein and Wayne Biggins. And in goal was veteran Peter Fox.

Peter Fox –
A man in desperate need of a haircut

Was this a surprise? Very much so. After years of service to Stoke, Fox found himself immediately sidelined by new manager Macari, who thought he was too old. However, Fox's many replacements were either cup-tied, injured, recalled loan players, or tied up in a cupboard. So, despite not playing a single league game, Fox played some Autoglass games, and all the League Cup games (including Liverpool), and all the FA Cup games (including bloody Telford!).

Did the game start well for Fox? Not particularly. Stockport had a goal disallowed for a foul on Fox, although Fox had to admit it wasn't a foul.

Lucky he wasn't the ref! Yeah, lucky that. Eventually, Stoke took control. Most of the long balls aimed at Francis never made it thanks to Overson and Cranson. Ironically, in the second half it was a long ball that reached Stein, who turned and slotted the ball home for 1-0.

What did the Stockport fans think of this? They reckoned the goal was "controversial", but they never say why. Mind you, they also claimed that "A fleet of coaches transported 20,000 County fans", when in fact it was nearer half that number, so I'm not sure where they're getting their facts from.

Another great victory at Wembley? If Stoke could only play all their away games there.

STOKE CITY VS BRISTOL CITY APRIL 2000

Was it a surprise for Stoke to find themselves back at Wembley eight years later in 2000? Yes, it was. This was mainly because Stoke thought they'd not get relegated to the lower divisions again, but then who'd have thought of putting Chris Kamara in charge knowing what we know now?

What was the competition called now? Fred.

And what was the competition *really* called now? OK, it was the Auto Windscreen Shield.

Were Stoke still in the South? No, they'd moved to the North part of the draw. With Gudjon Thordarsson as Stoke manager, they beat Darlington and Oldham with golden goals in extra time (3-2 and 1-0). Then they saw off Blackpool (2-1), Chesterfield (1-0), and Rochdale (3-1 & 1-0) to get to Wembley. It doesn't sound impressive now, and it wasn't so impressive then.

But Wembley...!? Yes, Bristol City didn't stand a chance really, and were beaten in an exciting 2-1 victory, with cracking goals from Graham Kavanagh and Peter Thorne. This was arguably a better game than the Stockport one, but it isn't mentioned so often, which is a shame.

Tony Pulis – he was never happy with this Bristol Rovers strip. Bristol City fans didn't like it either

Can we forget this competition now? Er, yes. Promotion two years later allowed Stoke to put this era behind them. Bristol had to put up with it for a few years longer.

So, who was managing Bristol City when they met Stoke at Wembley? Dunno, but for the first half of that season a man called Tony Pulis was manager, but he left immediately after beating Cheltenham 3-1 in the Auto Windscreen first round. He thought it wouldn't lead to anything, and he was right.

BLOODY PORT VALE!

Port Vale 0 Stoke City 1 (FA Cup)

8ᵗʰ January 1951

Are you talking about Stoke's neighbours, little Port Vale, struggling away at the bottom of League 2? Yeah, they're the ones. They're not so innocent.

Is this just an excuse to print old pictures of their long serving manager, John Rudge, now director of football at Stoke? OK, you got me.

Obligatory picture of a young happy John Rudge when he was at Bristol Rovers

And did you know that there are only 8 English cities that play "derby" matches involving teams from the same city? You don't say.

So how many times have Stoke met Port Vale in the FA Cup? Surprisingly only four times. Stoke first beat Vale 1-0 at home in 1887. It would have been 2-0, but a long-throw went straight into the net and was therefore disallowed.

Sounds like Rory Delap in a time-machine! He's not really Dr Who, is he? Curiously, neither Rory Delap nor The Doctor was on the Stoke team-sheet that day.

Can he take us forward in time in his TARDIS, please? Then, in 1922, Stoke visited the Potteries Shopping Centre car-park (in those days home to Vale's dilapidated Old Recreation Ground in Hanley) to beat Vale 4-2.

Chapter 9 - Vale

Who was Vale's player manager in those days? None other than (Dirty) Tommy Holford, former Stoke captain and owner of aforementioned droopy moustache (see his scary picture in the Introduction). It's believed that Tom holds the record of most appearances in Potteries derbies: 9 for Stoke, but 19 for Vale! Anyway, after that Stoke and Vale didn't meet again in the cup for nearly 30 years.

So, what happened in 1951 then? They met in the Third Round. 49,500 squeezed into the Victoria Ground, a potteries derby record crowd. Stoke were 8th in the top-flight, and had just done the double over Arsenal. Vale were in Division 3-South, and had just beaten New Brighton and Nelson (?!).

One way traffic? No. In fact, Vale went two up, but were pegged back to 2-2 in the second half. The replay was two days later. The Victoria Ground pitch may have resembled a bog after a bout of snow and rain, but the brand spanking new Vale Park and its freshly laid pitch was in an even worse state due to appalling drainage. So the replay was at Stoke's ground again.

More one way traffic? No, end to end stuff actually. The game was played on a Monday afternoon – neither club having floodlights, naturally. The game being as big as it was, workers were given time off to attend. However, light had begun to fade when Stoke scored the only goal two minutes from time. It was so dark by then that four players got lost on their way back to the dressing room (just kidding).

Did Stoke go on to win the cup? Sadly, after defeating West Ham, they met Newcastle United who put four past them in a 2-4 defeat.

What happened to Vale? They got thrown out of Division 3-South, and were moved to the more cushy Division 3-North. This happened a lot to Vale in those days. However, this move led to their promotion a few years later.

Chapter 9 - Vale

You're trying to avoid the other time that Stoke met Vale in the FA Cup, aren't you? OK! So they met again in the First Round in November 1992. Lou Macari and John Rudge were the managers by now, and Stoke and Vale were 2nd and 5th in the new 2nd Division (previously Division 3). Sky TV turned up with some giant Sumo wrestlers, although nobody quite knows why. Stoke had more of the game, with a disallowed goal and Mark Stein hitting the bar, but it ended 0-0. The replay at Vale Park was another matter.

Another matter? What, like Kryptonite? A bit. For starters, the Vale Park pitch was as bad as it was in 1952. The game should have been switched to the Victoria Ground. However, Vince Overson set up Lee Sandford to put Stoke in front, but Vale's Martin Foyle and Andy Porter made it 1-2 by half-time.

I thought Foyle and Porter weren't playing. Curiously, they weren't in the starting line-up for the first game, but were recalled for the replay.

Was it getting too dark to play? No, it was getting too wet to play. Dave Regis thought he'd equalised when he placed a shot into an empty goal, only for the ball to stop dead in the mud inches from the goal-line. Interesting.

Why interesting? Because when Stoke equalised in their 2-2 draw in 1951, the ball did exactly the same thing in the mud, only just *over* the goal-line. Anyway. Foyle ran off down the other end and made it 1-3, and Stoke were out.

Torquay's very own John Rudge

Did Vale go on to win the cup? Sadly, after defeating Altrincham, they met Newcastle United who put four past them in a 0-4 defeat.

Just like what happened to Stoke 40 years before! Eerie, eh?! Not really.

So what happened next? Er, nothing.

Yes, it did. Now what happened next? Stoke had won the Autoglass Trophy the year before. This time they met Vale in the southern area semi-final at the Victoria Ground. It was 3 months later, and Stoke were now top of the division with Vale second, so it was a real clash of the titans.

I feel a disaster coming on. For the record, Mark Stein missed a penalty, had a goal disallowed for offside, then missed an open goal. In fact, Stoke pounded Vale for the whole game. Finally, Van der Laan headed Vale's only goal.

I thought Van der Laan wasn't playing? He wasn't playing in the FA Cup games, but was recalled for this one. Typical. Vale then went on to win the trophy.

SUN SOCCERCARD No 121

Was there a happy ending for Stoke? A month later Stoke completed the double over Vale, breaking their home unbeaten record and ruining their promotion chances. Stoke finished champions. Vale crashed in the playoff final.

So Stoke can end on a high note here. Unfortunately, after Stoke got relegated again and beat Bristol City at Wembley, they found themselves playing Vale in 2001 in the *Northern* area Semi-Finals of the LDV Vans Trophy, as it was now called.

Why was it played at the Britannia Stadium? This time Vale Park really was unplayable, so due to a fixture backlog, the venue was switched. After 90 minutes it was 1-1 (2nd half goals from Michael Cummins and

L. MACARI (Scotland)

Teetotal Lou Macari –
a scary but sober man
(©News Group Newspapers)

then Nicky Mohan), so it went to golden goals. Vale won with a penalty from Bridge-Wilkinson after Mohan had handled. And yes, Vale went on to win the trophy, but promotion has proved more elusive. Relegation hasn't, though.

They need all the help they can get these days. Which is why we've sent them Micky Adams. It's the least we can do. The very least.

And the 8 English cities that play "derby" matches? London, Liverpool, Birmingham, Bristol, Nottingham, Sheffield, Manchester and Stoke. However, it looks like it could be some time before another potteries derby in the league. But an FA Cup potteries derby…? Now, wouldn't that be interesting?

BLOODY LIVERPOOL!

Stoke City 0 Liverpool 8 (Worthington Cup 4th round)

29th November 2000

What was it Martin Luther King said? I had a dream…a dream where I was at the Britannia Stadium in front of a sell-out crowd. Stoke were playing Liverpool, but everything was going wrong. They scored goal after goal, until the scoreboard could go no higher, sticking on 0-99. Then, just as their fans started up with You'll Never Walk Alone, we replied with Delilah and drowned them out.

Somebody had obviously been messing with the scoreboard

And Did Stoke then come back and win?! No, our keeper, Carl Muggleton, brought down Robbie Fowler, and he scored from the subsequent penalty.

OK, what really happened? Well, a week before all this Thordarson's Stoke had been beaten 0-1 by Nuneaton in the FA Cup. Bad news. Then a few days later, Port Vale crashed and burned at home to Canvey Island 1-2, which was very funny, particularly as Canvey were in the fairly obscure Ryman League.

So, Stoke were going to show Vale how to deal with Liverpool? And they started well enough with Peter Thorne missing an open goal, hitting the post in the 4th minute when it looked easier to score. Then it fell apart at the seams.

How apart did the seams fall? With the likes of Jamie Carragher, Robbie Fowler and Gary McAllister, goals rained in. By half-time it was 0-4. When Hypia made it 0-5, the home crowd started up with "We're going to win 6-5". At 0-7, the fans really did drown out the opposition with Delilah. When it got to 0-8, the scoreboard put up 0-9. By then Fowler had a hat-trick (from said penalty), and Liverpool had their highest ever away victory.

How did The Sentinel describe it? It was Stoke's worst defeat for 37 years. However, it's probably worse than that; Stoke's worst home defeat ever, and worse than losing away to Preston in 1889 by 0-10 (which is Stoke's worst ever defeat).

Whose fault was it? Tony Dorigo's.

Are you blaming it all on him because he was Australian? A bit harsh, but no. Tony was a defender and Stoke's skipper. To raise morale (?) he told everyone he was jinxed. He'd lost big games, such as losing a semi-final with Villa and a final with Leeds, and could see it in the tea-leaves it all happening again…although the PG Tips didn't predict 0-8. Tony also didn't predict the Liverpool fan running on to the pitch towards him. He thought he was being attacked, when in fact the fan had come to console him. A few weeks later he retired from football.

*Tony Dorigo
voodoo doll*

It didn't used to be like this. Although Stoke have never beaten Liverpool in the cup, the nearest they came was in 1991, when Macari's third division side almost knocked out Graeme Souness's bunch of misfits. Tony Kelly's late equaliser for Stoke at Anfield (2-2) left the second leg at the Victoria Ground wide open. But Tony Kelly's wobbly backpass gifted Liverpool an easy goal, and Stoke crashed out 2-3 on the night.

That was the nearest? No, sorry, the nearest Stoke have come to knocking Liverpool out of the cup was an FA Cup Third Round game in 1988, when Mick Mills' side were cruising to a 0-0 draw at Anfield when substitute Graham Shaw was put through in the last 5 minutes, but failed to beat the Liverpool keeper in a one-to-one.

This was no surprise? In the six FA Cups games these two clubs have played, Stoke have failed to score in any of them. Bear that in mind if Stoke draw them again in the future.

WHEN STOKE BEAT CHELSEA, MANCHESTER UNITED, ET AL!

Stoke City 6 Chelsea 2 (League Cup)

22nd October 1974

Right, once round the table. Any cup games we've forgotten? Chelsea.

Which game? Almost any you can think of. In the FA Cup they've met three times, always in the 5th round. Stan Matthews saw them off in 1934 with two goals in a 3-1 win. Chelsea then squeezed through in 1969 by 2-3. However, they met again in 2003, with Stoke bottom of the Championship and Chelsea 5th in the Premier. Despite Chelsea sporting the likes of Frank Lampard, John Terry & William Gallas, Stoke made it tough for them before going down 0-2.

What about the League Cup? Aha! Chelsea dread meeting Stoke in the League/Worthington/Rumbelows/Coca-Cola Cup. They've lost all four encounters. There was of course the 1972 Wembley bonanza. Then, as Chelsea started on their decline, Stoke beat them 1-0 in 1973 with a Denis Smith flying header – another cup defeat for Bonetti, Hudson, Osgood and Harris. Stoke followed this up the next year with two draws in the third round (2-2 and 1-1).

Who won the toss for the choice of venue for the next replay? Tony Waddington. Again! I reckon he had a two-sided coin. Even bet365 won't take bets from him!

And who won the game? Well, Stoke were 4-0 up at half-time, so that's a clue. Geoff Hurst got his second on 67 minutes to make it 6-0, but Stoke allowed two limp consolation goals to leave it 6-2. Of course, Alan Hudson was now with Stoke, and Chelsea's squad was seriously depleted. Stoke later beat them 3-0 at the end of the season, effectively sending them down.

And when they'd recovered…? When Chelsea had finally clawed their way into the Premier League in the early 1990s, starting their assent to their present league status, they faced Stoke in the Coca-Cola Cup in 1995. Macari's team of Sandford, Overson and Potter faced up to Glenn Hoddle's team of Ruud Gullit, Mark Hughes and Denis Wise. The spirited 0-0 draw at the Vic was followed by a dream 1-0 win at Stamford Bridge, with Paul Peschisolido (yes, the famous Burton Albion manager) popping up to score the only goal. Even Chelsea's star sub, Mark Stein, couldn't convert from 5 yards out.

Right, who's next? Manchester United.

Which cup game? Almost any. In the FA Cup, honours are fairly even, with 2 wins for Stoke and 3 for United, although they haven't met in the FA Cup since Stoke beat them in extra-time in 1972.

Are we better in the League Cup? United have only beaten Stoke once in 5 League Cup games. In 1993, they crossed swords again, when Macari's team of Cranson, Toddy Orlygsson and Mark Stein faced Ferguson's team of Bryan Robson, Mark Hughes and Dion Dublin. Although it wasn't United's strongest side (Eric Cantona in particular was resting with some poetry somewhere), they were still formidable. But Stoke outplayed them, with Stein scoring twice to secure a fantastic win by 2-1. In the second leg, Ferguson was forced to bring in the likes of Ryan Giggs, Lee Sharpe, Steve Bruce and Roy Keane.

"Off To The Match", by Sid Kirkham
(© Sid Kirkham, The ArtBay, Stoke-on-Trent)

Chapter 11 – Everybody else!

I thought they were all boring, grey-haired old managers. Well, Hughes, Bruce and Keane may be now, but they were at the top of their game then (albeit still boring). But for this game, they made little difference, and United just scraped home with a late goal to win 0-2, or 2-3 on aggregate.

Did this performance change anything? Ruin for United? Ultimate triumph for Stoke? It didn't change much. United went on to win the league and cup double that season. Within three weeks of this game Stoke had lost Macari, Stein and any chance of making the playoffs.

Anyone else? Arsenal?

Is it worth bothering with them? Probably not. Stoke have never beaten them in the cup. After the debacle of the 1971/1972 semi-finals, Stoke have lost twice to Arsenal in the FA Cup in close games. In 1990, Alan Ball's Stoke were bottom of the 2nd Division whilst Arsenal were 3rd in the top-flight. However, it took a late goal by the current chairman of Sunderland (Niall Quinn) to knock Stoke out. In 2005, Arsenal came from behind to win 1-2, with Wayne Thomas scoring for Stoke and Robin van Persie volleying the winner. Only Steve Simonsen remains at Stoke from that team.

You seem to be dismissing these games a bit easily. Maybe. But with Stoke back in the Premier League, these upsets seem to dim slightly in the memory. Why remember when Stoke almost beat Arsenal, when now they can beat them 2-1 in the league. OK, so Macari's teams beat Chelsea and Manchester United, but similar wins under Tony Pulis seem near enough to touch.

So what are Stoke's chances of winning cups under Tony Pulis? Well, he started off promisingly in his first season at Stoke (2002/03) in the FA Cup,

Tony Pulis (centre) blasts home for Newport County

beating Wigan and his-old-team-Bournemouth before courageously going down to Chelsea 0-2 (see above). Since then it's been speedy exits to

Wimbledon, Arsenal, Fulham, Newcastle United, and Hartlepool United. Hm.

More chance in the League (Carling) Cup? You wouldn't have thought so, with early round defeats to Gillingham, Oldham, Darlington and Rochdale. But with that track record, reaching the quarter-finals in 2008 was pretty astonishing; Stoke hadn't been that far since the 1970s.

And who did they lose to? Only Derby County, which is where we came in, if you remember, back in 1899.

Any other games we've missed? The FIVE games against Bury in 1955 – lunacy. The disallowed penalty on Lee Dixon against Coventry in 1987 - travesty. The many annoying defeats by lower division Burnley – revenge is coming, don't you worry.

BLACKMAIL CORNER - £10,000 in used notes or I reveal who this is playing for Bristol Rovers. Send money to The Tony Pulis Blackmail Quiz, at......oh damn!

So, are Stoke going to win the FA Cup this season? Yep. And this is how:

- **Third Round: Blyth Spartans 0 Stoke 5** – TV cameras turn up in hope of upset, only to see Blyth go three down after 12 minutes. Blyth's local postman (also their left-back) turns up 10 minutes late and misses the first two goals. Shame.
- **Fourth Round: Port Vale 0 Stoke City 0** – Vale's pitch is worse than ever. Tony Pulis plays 5 at the back just in case. The gate stops Vale going under.

- **Replay: Stoke City 4 Port Vale 0** – a packed Brit sees Vale given the push in style. But at least Vale can now afford to pay their water rates.
- **Fifth Round: Stoke City 2 Liverpool 1** –Liverpool have it all sewn up at 0-1, before Fuller scores a late brace. He becomes the only player EVER to score for Stoke against Liverpool in the FA Cup.
- **Sixth Round: Derby County 0 Stoke City 1** – Nosebleeds all round: Stoke haven't been this far in nearly 40 years, so Tony Pulis plays SIX players across the back. Somehow they score.
- **Semi-final: Arsenal 1 Stoke City 2** – Arsenal have three goals disallowed for offside, concede a goal from a corner that should have been a goal-kick, then concede a penalty that only the referee sees. How unlucky is that? Arsene Wenger this time really does have something to moan about. But do we care? I don't think so.
- **Final: Portsmouth 1 Stoke City 3** – Harry Redknapp is back managing Pompey YET AGAIN after getting the push from Spurs. Tony Pulis shows him who is the master now.

So there you are. All of Stoke City's cup dramas. Indeed. But let's be optimistic, the best cup games are ahead of us.

Can we go down the pub now? We ARE down the pub. Don't you remember, they locked us in and boarded up the windows.

Can't we go home then? Hang on, I think I've got the Sky TV box to work…

Acknowledgements

Where possible, permission for reproducing material has been sought, and we thank the many generous people and organisations who have allowed us to use this material (including Bob Bond, Philip Neill & Sid Kirkham). Apologies to any organisation that we've missed or we were just unable to trace. Furthermore, we have striven to ensure that all is factual, and hope that you agree that we have been fair in our appraisal Thanks to Poolie and all the "Al"s down the pub. For Shell, Ad, Bek & Dyl.